# Reengineering Purchasing

# Reengineering Purchasing

## *Lessons from the Front Lines*

Paul D. Ericksen

**BEP**

BUSINESS EXPERT PRESS

*Leader in applied, concise business books*

Reengineering Purchasing: Lessons from the Front Lines

Cover design by Gregory Paus

Interior design by S4Carlisle Publishing Services, Chennai, India

First published in 2025 by
Business Expert Press, LLC
222 East 46th Street, New York, NY 10017
www.businessexpertpress.com

ISBN-13: 978-1-63742-844-3 (paperback)
ISBN-13: 978-1-63742-845-0 (e-book)

Business Expert Press Supply and Operations Management Collection

First edition: 2025

10 9 8 7 6 5 4 3 2 1

**EU SAFETY REPRESENTATIVE**
Mare Nostrum Group B.V.
Mauritskade 21D
1091 GC Amsterdam
The Netherlands
gpsr@mare-nostrum.co.uk

# Testimonials

*Drawing on personal experience from a long, successful career in purchasing, Ericksen shows how you can turn zero-sum negotiations into win-win results. He is a thought leader in progressive supply chain strategy and practice.*—**Professor Josh Whitford, Associate Professor of Sociology, and Co-Director of the Idea Lab on Firms and Industrial Policy in the Center for Political Economy, Columbia University**

*Ericksen provides urgently needed lessons learned that expand the scope and positive financial impact of corporate purchasing. He explains how the function can produce better financial impact by transitioning from a Fordist commodity procurement approach to one more suited to today's business challenges. A must-read for purchasing managers and corporate executives.*—**Dr. Matt Vidal, Associate Professor of Sociology, Loughborough University**

*With a storyteller's charm, Paul Ericksen turns purchasing tradition on its head, moving from 'we've always done it this way' to 'here's how we can excel together.' He skillfully reshapes leadership perspectives, transforming suppliers into strategic allies. A delightfully insightful guidebook for up-and-coming change agents.*—**Ryan Kelly, Vice-President of Technology, Association for Manufacturing Technology**

# About the Author

**Paul D. Ericksen** spent 18 years working in supply management at large corporations, starting out as a Technical Buyer and ending up serving a stint as Chief Procurement Officer at a Fortune 300 corporation. Consequently, he knows the "ins and outs" across the range of purchasing roles. He later spent 10 years working as an executive level consultant.

Paul is a well-known writer and speaker on supply management issues, including a role as Supply Chain Advisor to IndustryWeek's and the Center for Advanced Procurement. He also served as Chairman of the Board of several multiple state and national supply chain related programs. For his work in economic improvement, he has received special recognition from the governor of State of Wisconsin and The Modernization Forum.

In his book Reengineering Purchasing: Lessons From The Front Lines, Ericksen shares over three dozen personal experiences where he was responsible for fundamental change to purchasing strategy and practice that increased the competitiveness of the companies and clients he worked at and for. At the end of each chapter are listed the lessons learned from each experiences.

Paul has pioneered an extended enterprise approach to management of strategic suppliers, which is based on gaining win-win results for both parties. This counters with the positional win-lose approach used today by many corporations. His stories show how a more collaborative approach increases the positive financial impact purchasing can contribute above-and-beyond piece-price reduction.

The book will benefit anyone working in supply management, as well as corporate executives looking for a new and expanded approach to purchasing.

# Contents

## Part 3

# Acknowledgments

I owe a lot to the people who—both throughout my life and career—supported and mentored me in my endeavors. I also owe significant debt to those whom I supported and mentored, since this led to significant personal and professional growth making me who I am today.

First and foremost, though, it was my wife Cindy who, throughout my career, was always there for me. She "had my back" when I needed it and acted as a sounding board, giving me advice on important decisions I needed to make. Cindy was always there to encourage and support me when I needed it most. Thanks, Dear.

# PART 1

# Introduction

It was primarily in the 1960s that my fundamental persona was molded. I grew up in Iowa, an Upper-Midwest State. I can say that back then there were basic tenets that contributed to people's value system there, and you'd hear—at least you did relative to people of my generation—that Upper-Midwesterners were hard working people who relied on their own efforts—not taking advantage of others—to achieve success.

This is called *having ethics*.

It is my experience that—at least for the most part—such ethics don't exist in the culture of today's corporate world. This began with Milton Friedman's assertion—made in the late 1970s—that a public company's sole focus should be on maximizing profits, thus increasing shareholder value. In other words, corporations will no longer adhere to the betterment of the traditional *three-legged-stool* of stakeholders: ownership, employees/suppliers, and community.

This strategy has now gained near universal acceptance in business, which has been translated into a philosophy that values short-term *win-lose* profitability. If you doubt this, you might want to listen to a company's quarterly stock analyst update. You'll likely find the analysts aren't really interested in hearing about longer-term company initiatives.

Besides the obvious, this philosophy has greatly affected change management within corporations. In today's business environment, short-term changes to increase profitability with the losers often their own employees and suppliers are the typical approach to change management. This has been counterproductive to ongoing company competitiveness since it usually leads to Incremental improvements—that is, tweaking—which is easily replicated and implemented by competitors.

Related to this, there have been significant impacts on corporate culture. In one case, it has led to a dearth of mentors in corporations with either the experience or motivation to teach younger employees how to justify and implement changes that will lead to significant, longer-term positive impacts on marketplace competitiveness.

The reason for writing this book is to lay out my experiences as a *change agent*, which, hopefully, will provide guidance to anyone wishing to take this career path. The primary area of my work experience was in purchasing. I worked for two major corporations and then transitioned to a successful 10-year consulting career. Among others, my clients included multiyear engagements with two Fortune 100 corporations.

Unfortunately, during that career, I typically found that executive management considered the main—and sometimes only—positive financial contribution that the purchasing function could make to their organization's bottom line was in reducing purchased material cost. And there was an assumption and the expectation that purchasing could most effectively lower costs by taking advantage of suppliers through zero-sum positional negotiations.

This ties directly into my previous comments about ethics. In other words, original equipment manufacturers (OEMs) today are taking advantage of others to achieve their own business success.

I started working in purchasing in 1988 and experienced my employer becoming more and more focused on increasing stock price, that is, shareholder wealth. It was almost stunning to see how quickly the changes in purchasing strategy and processes began to align with Milton Friedman's business philosophy.

For instance, this focus on supplier price reduction was integrated into personnel and departmental performance metrics—with very little regard for anything else—which discouraged purchasing personnel from proposing and/or implementing changes that had the potential—over time—to deliver significantly higher positive financial impacts than those that could be achieved by chasing lower prices.

For instance, *true* lead-time—lead-time not achieved through waste such as prebuilt, prepositioned finished goods inventory—is a metric that ties directly to successfully supporting market demand, that is, increasing sales. Yet, it is not used as a metric by virtually any corporation—at least not to my knowledge—during source selection.

I found it was against my personal values to operate within such a *win-lose* structure. You might think that this had been a strong barrier toward career success. It wasn't, as seen by my progress up the organizational ladder, starting out as a Technical Buyer and ending up as a Chief Procurement Officer.

This advancement was achieved through operating as a *change agent* through actions such as:

- Assisting suppliers in identifying and reducing their own internal waste.
- Increasing supplier ability to better support the demand dynamics of the markets their OEM customer(s) participated in.
- Setting individual annual supplier price reduction goals based on their current *Leanness*.
- Starting up a supplier development function and other infrastructure needed as a resource for supporting these actions.

For instance, there is less cost-reduction potential with Lean suppliers than there is with those that are less Lean. Cost-reduction targets should recognize this disparity. Along these same lines, it is wrong to assume that suppliers have more waste than their OEM customers. Based on this, where appropriate, it seems that supplier annual cost-reduction goals should be related to those of their OEM customer.

This is not to say I wasn't aggressive in setting supply chain performance goals. But they were set such that suppliers had a realistic chance of achieving them, as opposed to unrealistic across-the-board *pie-in-the-sky* cost-reduction expectations that, by the way, are rarely met.

Bottom line, it makes a lot more sense for OEMs to help their suppliers Lean up than by pushing them more toward anorexia through win-lose negotiations. But most don't. Why? Because for the most part corporations adhere rigidly to a Milton Friedman–inspired business strategy. But perhaps more importantly, corporations are risk resistant for fear of failure. If you doubt this, ask yourself why so many *startups* are able to sell their products, and themselves, to OEMs. In other words, while in the past OEMs tended to do their own research and development of new strategies and tools, today that approach seems to be the exception rather than the rule.

I was somewhat taken aback at my retirement party to find that—in addition to company colleagues—several supplier owners and principals were in attendance. At one point in the evening, they came up to me as a group and gave me what I consider the highest compliment of my professional career, which was along the lines of:

*Paul, you set high standards for us but unlike other customers, showed us how to—and assisted us in—meeting them. Working with you did not make us feel like we we're operating in a zero-sum game.*

Another comment that was made that evening was:

*Paul, you operated like an old-time Materials Manager, leaving meat-on-the-bone for your suppliers. As a result, we were more committed to helping you than any of our other customers.*

And the basis of the above comments was simply that I operated as a *change agent* in—at least in what I hoped—was an ethical win-win manner.

I guess my kinder-garden teacher had it right when she wrote in my end-of-year report card:

*Paul has a decided sense of what is right and wrong. He is more than willing to do his share if he believes he is right.*

I wish that everyone felt the same way in both their personnel and professional lives but, in my experience, few do.

You'll see in reading this book that much about what I learned in becoming a *change agent* was through experiences at the *school of hard knocks.*

Part 1 of this work will lay out the background in which I had to operate—as well as specific functions/individuals in the corporate hierar-chy that hindered my efforts—and how they were dealt with.

Part 2, the bulk and *meat* of this work, will outline a multitude of ·eer experiences where a decision had to be made whether or not to k to change an existing strategy and/or process to achieve competitive
ntage.

Part 3 will provide a final wrap-up including a significant case study, as well as detailed explanation of two important concepts relative to this book.

Due to my background, these experiences will be grouped from engagements I had that either touched on or were directly related to the purchasing function. As detailed in the following points, they will be laid out in sequential order based on the stage in my career that they occurred:

- As a Quality Engineer
- As a Technical Buyer
- As a Materials Manager
- As a Chief Procurement Officer (CPO)
- As an Executive-Level Consultant.

Due to its span of control—as well as the several years I held the position—the bulk of the changes that I witnessed occurred during my tenure as a Materials Manager.

At the end of each chapter, I will summarize the experience. Next, I will rate the change as *No Change, Incremental, Evolutionary*, or *Revolutionary*, as well as the reason for the rating. Then I will list the *Lessons Learned* from the experience.

You'll note that there is repetition with some of the lessons learned, such as "Don't allow yourself to be bullied." But most make points related wholly to a specific experience.

It is my hope reading this book will give insight on how purchasing personnel and, for that matter, an individual working in any corporate functional area can act as a *change agent*, identifying and championing change that will positively impact company competitiveness.

I also hope that the stories will help to understand how to break down the *purchasing silo* within your organization.

Enjoy.

Paul D. Ericksen

# Background

# CHAPTER 1

# Change Management

*The times, they are—or should be—a changin'.*

## The Essence of Change

It is unreasonable to expect an increase in competitive advantage without changes being made to current company strategies and processes. Being a *change agent* implies that in addition to your current *status quo* duties, you look to justify and implement changes that will increase company competitiveness in a quantifiable and ongoing way.

During my career I was involved in many changes that greatly increased purchasing's contribution to my employer's bottom line. There is no doubt in my mind that such opportunities continue to exist.

My perspective is that there are three primary types of change management, which are as follows:

1. **Incremental:** Changes that do not significantly vary from current practice and are easily justified and implemented. These types of changes do not deliver meaningful financial results and, at best, deliver a minimal, short-term competitive advantage since they can easily be discerned and replicated by competitors. Another way to describe the Incremental change process is *tweaking*.

   Incremental changes expose the company to minimal risk of not delivering the projected outcome(s) and require minimal resources to implement. Incremental change initiatives usually do not require approval from management.

   An example of an Incremental change was when purchasing transitioned from sending out requests for quote (RFQs) and receiving supplier pricing proposals by paper to doing so electronically.

While I'm sure there were corporations that led the way in this transition, it only delivered minimal, short-term competitive advantage since competitors easily recognized and implemented the same change.

2. **Evolutionary:** Changes that—while they are based on current practice—vary from them in a meaningful way. This type of change delivers positive and quantifiable financial impacts. They provide longer periods of competitive advantage than tweaking since competitors will require a longer period of time to both notice and increase their effort to implement similar changes.

   Evolutionary changes are more difficult to justify and require more resources to implement. Their justification typically takes the form as a business case—possibly based upon *Proof-of-Concept* pilot results—and requires a certain level of management approval. There is risk associated with Evolutionary change that increases the further one deviates from a current practice.

   An example of an Evolutionary change was when corporations transitioned from disposable to returnable shipping containers. Here, the waste elimination, labor reduction, and associated streamlining part access to an assembly line are easily quantified. While the change would be noticed by competitors, their own installation of it will be longer due to the need to design and manufacture containers tailored for specific products and assemblies, as well as the need to justify a significant capital investment.

3. **Revolutionary**: Changes that have few or no ties to current practice. They represent a totally new approach to fundamental business strategies and processes and, as such, need to be justified through the development of a rigorous business case to gain executive management approval. High-level sponsorship should be sought for Revolutionary change initiatives to prevent them from being stonewalled and/or cancelled.

An example of a Revolutionary change is when a corporation adopts *true* lead-time as a factor in source selection. A shorter lead-time implies a *Leaner* (lower waste), more progressive supplier. When applied to a critical mass of suppliers, it can also lead to a supplier base that can more quickly respond to changes in market dynamics, resulting in increased overall sales and profitability. Another way to describe such a supply-base is World-Class. In my mind, facilitating the development of a World-Class Supply-Base should be the Number 1 goal all purchasing functions.

## A Manager's Leadership Role

Managers are expected to competently tend to issues within their personal span of control. Perhaps more importantly, though, they are expected to develop into *leaders*. Just being placed in a position of authority doesn't make someone a leader. Such stature is something that needs to be earned. In my mind, the litmus test for whether a manager is a leader, or not, is their approach to change management.

I've always been a *change agent*. I guess it is part of my DNA. Over my career, I was effective at putting together solid business case justifications for—and implementing—significant changes that positively impacted my employer's and/or consulting client's bottom line in a quantifiable way.

Implementing significant change is not easy and can categorize a manager. Many years ago, I received sage advice that has stuck with me. It takes the form of the following three leadership categories:

- A *Manager* is someone who is perceived as favoring the status quo. Because of this—when they advocate change—it is usually Incremental.
- A *Lunatic* is someone who is perceived as being at least one-step-ahead of everyone else. This implies that they primarily promote Evolutionary changes.
- A *Heretic* is someone who is perceived as being at least two steps ahead of everyone else. Their focus is primarily on Revolutionary change.

This advice was an epiphany for me. It helped me understand that managers fit into specific categories based on their organization's perception of their approach to change—and that the larger the change, the higher the risk of criticism, and higher the probability of significant reward.

## Incremental Managers

Status quo managers focus on the easiest and least risky form of change. Don't get me wrong—Incremental changes are necessary. But they should be considered as something that is *necessary but not sufficient* relative to increasing company competitiveness.

Those who rely solely on this type of strategy *may* be capable of thinking outside of their own box but, due to fear of failure, usually don't. Consequently, while their focus on Incremental change may help satisfy their personal performance metrics, they seldom improve company competitiveness in a quantifiable way. Such individuals fall to the bottom of my leadership assessment. I have never hired or promoted one.

## Evolutionary Managers

One-step-ahead managers primarily focus on Evolutionary change. They streamline and/or otherwise improve current practices that deliver a significant, quantifiable competitive advantage that has a certain amount of staying power.

My assessment of Evolutionary managers is very positive. I enjoy working with people who try to expand the limits of current practice.

## Revolutionary Managers

Effective two-steps-ahead managers are few and far between but, when found, should be highly valued. The changes they succeed in making don't just change business: *They create new ways of doing business.*

The one caution I would make relative to such leaders is that they should carefully pick their battles when considering areas for change and *stick with proposing those that have the highest probability of success.* Failed change initiatives lower the probability that your future proposals for Evolutionary and/or Revolutionary change will be supported. Early successes can have an opposite, positive effect. Another way of looking at this is that successful instances of Incremental and Evolutionary change will open the way for executive acceptance of Revolutionary change proposals.

## Change Agents

Being a *change agent* won't necessarily endear you to colleagues, especially those who made their mark by creating *existing states*. But at the end of a career—and I suspect life in general—it will be these major accomplishments that give you the greatest satisfaction.

A follow-up observation is probably worth making. *Change agents* are seldom satisfied in either working or staying in a functional area managed by an Incremental manager. I don't perceive people who do as high-potential employees.

I was once fortunate to have put together a nine-person supplier development group comprised of high-potential individuals. I was criticized by some for hiring all of them from outside of the company. However, the master's level industrial engineering program they had graduated from was closely aligned with the delivery of the type of supplier development support needed to deliver changes that would support my employer's business strategies.

All made significant contributions to the success of our supplier development engagements and were recognized internally to the point where all nine were promoted to other departments 2 to 3 years after being initially hired—a very unusual occurrence. After that, I had the pick of internal candidates, a multitude that would make it known that they were interested in any openings within in my organization. This allowed for the maintenance of a high-performing work team.

## Summary

The role of a *change agent* should be to championing changes in strategy and practice that will significantly improve the competitiveness of their company in a quantifiable and enduring way. This will usually require they work out of their comfort zone.

Upfront justification of a change proposal is a critical step to both justifying to yourself and to your bosses' that a change initiative is merited, especially in the case of Evolutionary or Revolutionary change. So is a track record of previous successful change.

It is important to have the employees you will rely on for initiating success to be well qualified in both education and background for a change to be successful.

## Change Rating

*Revolutionary*, since I have never seen managers and other personnel categorized based on their effectiveness as a *change agent*.

## Lesson Learned

- A manager's value to an organization should be based—at least in part—on the positive impacts on company competitiveness due to the changes they propose and successfully implement. This should also play a role in assessing a person's promotability.
- There needs to be a motivating factor to create a culture of change within an organization. This usually requires adding change management goals to both employee and departmental performance.
- Regardless of leadership, the employees who do the work determine the success or failure of implementing a change, particularly those who are in the "Evolutionary" or "Revolutionary" category. Consequently, hiring or otherwise staffing personnel should have both the specific education and work experiences that will lead to implementation success.

# CHAPTER 2

# Are Ethics Possible in Corporate America?

As outlined in the Introduction, I believe there is a generational lack of ethics in Corporate America. This is because the previous traditional three-legged-stool of stakeholders—ownership, employees/suppliers, and communities—has been replaced by a sole focus on increasing shareholder wealth through increasing stock price and, often unsaid but true, tying executive compensation to those increases.

As can be seen from the above, I believe that in the three-legged stool structure suppliers should be considered part of the employee leg since, over the last couple of generations, much of what had previously been fabricated in-house by OEM employees has been outsourced to suppliers. Correspondingly, OEMs—in the same way that they have worked to impose reduced pay and benefits on their current employees—have also set unreasonable annual price reduction goals for their suppliers that lower the compensation of *their* employees.

And executives wonder why people entering the workforce today are less and less interested in a manufacturing job than a generation ago.

## Win-Win, or Win-Lose: To Be or Not to Be

The present OEM strategy for purchased material cost reduction is, in my mind, an example of unethical and counterproductive behavior. Why? Because it is based on a win-lose negotiating strategy that, while it may be effective in the short run, is not effective over time. If you dispute this, just consider General Electric and Boeing.

Many reading this book may say that this is an unfair assessment. In other words, they believe their company does work with their suppliers in a collaborative win-win manner.

To this I say, ask your supplier's opinion on this issue. I have seen in my consulting years that a vast majority of those I talked to replied with an emphatic **no**. That's what they'd likely tell you if they believed there would be no negative repercussions.

An example of the OEM win-lose approach is in how they structure their annual supplier material cost-reduction goals. The plain truth is that they tend to be unrealistically high. For instance, it was not unusual to see OEMs set them at 5 percent. And this is when their own internal annual cost reductions goals are in the range of 2 percent or less! Does this make sense? Of course not! Do OEMs really think their suppliers are less Lean than they are themselves? If so, is this based on factual data or assumption?

If you do the math, you'll find that if a purchased part stayed in production for 5 years (not an unreasonable expectation) that a 5 percent annual price-reduction goal—at level commonly set by OEMs—would require a supplier to sell to their OEM customer parts at about 82 percent of the price that they had quoted to gain the business in the first place. Most suppliers I've dealt with don't have 18 percent of waste to eliminate, especially when their own raw material cost makes up a significant part of their pricing. Consequently, many suppliers end up having to reduce margins in order to keep current business.

Similar calculations relative to the OEM's typical internal 2 percent annual cost-reduction goals would yield a 5-year cost reduction to about 92 percent of the original cost, which I believe is realistic and would be an appropriate purchased material cost-reduction goal. *Do as I say, not as I do* is usually not a good motivator; nor would it seem to endear an OEM to its supply-base.

Since we're talking about a lack of ethics in OEM management of their supply chain *partners*, I'll ask you what you think happens when they are constantly asked by their customers to deliver unrealistic price reductions? Believe me when I tell you, they don't like it and feel it is hypocritical. And like with company culture, once you impose a strictly commercial relationship with what is supposed to be a partner supplier, it's difficult to reestablish collaboration.

At those same lines, the Chief Executive Officer (CEO) of a former employer of mine was once quoted in the August 14, 2007 edition of *The Wall Street Journal* as saying that one of the major problems he was having to deal with was there being *too much of a family feeling* among company employees.

In my mind, this comment also implied criticism to collaborative management of suppliers.

At the time, my employer was in the midst of setting several consecutive years of record profits, due in part to increases in employee productivity and working collaboratively with suppliers on cost reduction. How's that for high performance?

Perhaps it was because employees and suppliers were working as a *team*, or as the CEO put it, a *family*.

I guess the CEO wanted employees competing against each other rather than working together. In my mind, this is not an ethical approach to managing employees.

At the time, I wondered how the CEO's position lined up with company's basic core values, which were and are documented as *Integrity*, *Quality*, *Commitment*, and *Innovation*. My conclusion was that they didn't.

## Performance Metrics

There is no performance metric that I am aware of for ethical behavior, and perhaps because of this, it does not seem to be on the radar screen of today's company executives and their employees. Given how much corporations tout their own ethical and moral behavior, it is confusing why they aren't evaluated in these areas.

One final word on ethics. I mentioned earlier that a corporate focus on short-term stock performance benefited stockholders *and* executive management. This is because Boards-of-Directors have, over the last couple of decades, transitioned from awarding executive's monetary bonuses to granting them stock options as an incentive to focus on increasing stock price. Need I mention that many Directors on company Boards are also compensated in stock options. Needless to say, this is an unethical conflict of interests.

If you were an executive, how would you operate under such a reward system? Unfortunately, too many respond by laying off employees and hiring part-timers as replacements; outsourcing work to foreign suppliers; cutting employee overall compensation; and, using *windfall profits* to buy back company stock to the sole purpose of increasing stock price.

# Summary

Operating in Corporate America today can challenge the maintenance of personnel ethics. I once heard a long-term purchasing veteran say that working in supply management can be a *soul-losing* proposition. In my mind, that statement doesn't seem too far off.

Although OEMs are reluctant to share in the windfall "good times," I have seen many *Dear Supplier* letters conveying the organization's "everyone-must-share-the-pain" position during business downturns. This is certainly an example of unethical—or at least hypocritical—behavior.

I understand that there are instances where purchasing personnel must go along with what are seemingly unpalatable company actions. But this should only be when not doing so would negatively influence the viability of the overall organization. Employees should not be asked to do this as part of an overall business strategy.

# Change Rating

No change was involved here, hence no Change Rating.

# Lessons Learned

- It is unfortunate to say that if a person's motivation is based strictly on increasing their compensation, they are a good fit for today's corporate culture.
- I once had a near-death experience. Believe me when I say that at the potential end-of-life, more thought is given to both decisions and actions you regret than the amount of money you've accrued.
- Ethics need to be included in evaluating employee performance as a first step in changing company culture. This is because without incenting ethical behavior, many employees will put self-interest above doing what is right for the company, supply-base, and end-use customers.

# CHAPTER 3

# Organizational Impact on Change Management

A purchasing's reporting hierarchy is a significant factor in whether the function is considered tactical or strategic, each having either a positive or negative impact on the ability to implement change. I'll discuss the more common structures below.

## Unit Material Managers

My all-time-favorite job was as an *Independent* Unit Materials Manager. Why? Because *local* management can better tailor strategies and processes to most effectively support the needs of the end-use customer. From a personnel perspective, I believe that all Unit and corporate performance metrics should be market driven.

Material managers are usually allowed to make their own decisions as to whether to proceed with either Incremental change or Evolutionary change. This means that initiative-related decisions can be made in short order and that minimum executive oversight is required as changes are implemented.

## Divisional Managers

This structure can have a negative impact on supplier management strategies and processes since it moves change one step away from an end-use customer. On the other hand, products produced within a Division may have design commonality, implying it could make sense to have some overlap in supplier selection and management.

Such collaboration, however, only makes sense if the market-demand characteristics of those various products also overlap.

For instance, if the product produced at one Unit has consistent or unchanging annual demand—while that manufactured at another has demand that is highly seasonal—it may be necessary to source with suppliers having different agility capabilities to ensure the most effective overall order fulfillment support.

Another differentiating factor may be in the time a customer is willing to wait for an out-of-stock product, due to product complexity and/or whether that product is targeted for consumer or commercial markets. Consumers will seldom wait long if a product is currently not available.

A Divisional hierarchy means that decisions to proceed with Evolutionary change or Revolutionary change will probably require approval by a Division Director or Vice-President. In today's corporate culture, such approvals are usually dependent whether or not it will have a positive, short-term financial impact.

## Non-Purchasing Executives

This structure represents a bad situation for a potential *change agent*. Why? For at least two reasons. First, it is an indicator that the overall organization undervalues the purchasing function. Because of this, it treats purchasing as tactical. Under such an organizational structure, purchasing ends up reporting to an individual who has little or no awareness of current purchasing strategies, processes, and current supply-base status.

At one time, I worked in a purchasing organization that reported to a Product Engineering Vice-President who, in turn, reported the Vice-President of Manufacturing. This type or organization made no sense and put a damper on the organizational perception of the value of the purchasing function. My perception at the time was that the Manufacturing VP was working to create an "empire" that would position himself toward becoming the Division's next President.

For instance, I once attended a get-together of Divisional management where I overheard a conversation between the Product Engineering

Vice-President and his two Directors. One of the Directors made the following statement to the other two, somewhat along the lines of:

*I don't understand why purchasing promotes the idea that the function is complicated, requiring extensive education and experience. When I need a new pair of shoes I tell my wife the style, color, and brand I want. She then looks to find—and buy—the lowest priced option. Isn't that the type of relationship that purchasing should have with product engineering and the company's suppliers?*

This perception is absurdly wrong and confirms my contention that other functional areas don't really understand the ins and outs of purchasing strategies or processes.

In the above case, the VP of Manufacturing valued the purchasing function even less. One consequence of this was to disregard any type of concerns and/or proposed changes coming from purchasing. In order to be an effective—and successful—*change agent*, I often had to *hide* change proposals from my Divisional chain-of-command until a Proof-of-Concept *pilot* had been run that delivered indisputable positive financial results.

## Finance

This is by far the worst reporting structure for a *change agent* to operate in. A 2014 column written in *IndustryWeek* by (then) executive editor Pat Panchak—**Did Finance Gut Manufacturing?**—had a thought-provoking title that, I'm sure, raised the hackles of any financial people who may have read it. You only need to think about how finance penalizes manufacturing costs for *reducing* lot sizes to align with current demand—a primary strategy of Lean production—to understand what she was getting at.

Panchak's column went on to outline how manufacturing reporting to finance typically has a detrimental impact to an organization's overall bottom line.

She also made the same argument relative to a reporting structure where purchasing reports to a Chief Financial Officer (CFO). In doing so, she quoted Marty Thomas, then Senior Vice-President of Operations and Engineering Services for Rockwell Automation:

> *If you have strategic sourcing reporting to finance, what do you get? You get purchase price reduction. What else do you get? Nothing. You get purchase price [reduction] at all costs. You don't get lead-time; you don't get order quantity; you don't get on-time delivery, and you don't get quality. You get purchase price reduction. You get what you deserve.*

I agree completely with Thomas's outlook on this. I could also add to Mr. Thomas's quote by saying you don't get either supplier or internal overhead reduction or effective supplier market support.

Where did this emphasis on price reduction come from?

Part of the answer is The New York Stock Exchange. For public companies, CFOs are expected to provide stock analysts quarterly reviews of profitability and forecast stock prices for succeeding quarters. If stock prices align with or exceed what was previously projected for a specific company, analysis *may* give a *buy* recommendation for their stock, which tends to raise its price. If they do not, analysts typically will give a *sell* recommendation, which tends to lower its price.

It does not require much of a leap of logic to make the point that CFOs, too, report to a type of outside financial function!

Investors today have expectations that their stocks will appreciate significantly over the short-term. As a result—as previously stated but bears repeating—rather than applying the more traditional recognition of employees, suppliers, and communities as equal stakeholders to ownership, corporate emphasis now almost exclusively focuses on investor interests.

And again, when corporations have cash surpluses, they tend to apply them to stock buybacks, which reduce the number of outstanding shares and, consequently, raise the price of those that remain.

It is a fact that changes to purchasing strategy and process can reduce or eliminate OEM internal costs, something not in the purview of CFOs. I have yet to meet a CFO who understands the intricacies of purchasing and supplier capabilities or acknowledges that purchasing can be more than a cost center. Supplier ability can also facilitate increased sales when forecasts do not align with market demand.

## Corporate Control

Another organization structure is when a company adopts a centralized purchasing organization managed by a Chief Procurement Officer (CPO). The company I worked for hired its first CPO from another organization. This person significantly overpromised the results he could deliver, probably telling the Board of Directors what he thought he needed to in order to get the job.

He then brought in four individuals to fill—also from outside the company—four newly created Director positions. They did not—or even seem—to care about understanding the importance of the relationship between *true* lead-time and variation in demand for Unit products, existing suppliers' supply chain flexibility capability, or suppliers critical to Unit and/or Divisional success. Pretty much all they brought to the company was a solitary focus on win-lose negotiations. They also resisted all change and/or deviations from this approach.

## A Telling Survey Result

A 2022 Survey of OEMs by the Center for Advanced Purchasing Studies showed that only 12 percent of CPOs reported directly to their CEO; 65 percent reported to a function that then reported to the CEO; and 19 percent reported through two functions below the CEO. This is a strong indication that at most corporations purchasing indeed is considered a tactical position. In other words, purchasing does not have a seat at the table when corporate strategies and goals are set. This is not good.

Why? Because the further the responsibility for purchasing is from the Unit level, the lesser the probability that source selection and management will increase the competitiveness of the products produced there.

## Summary

A manager should be evaluated not only on successfully optimizing current strategy and practice, but perhaps even more so on the changes made to those strategies and practices that—in a quantifiable way—significantly increase company competitiveness. Its position in the corporate reporting hierarchy heavily influences purchasing's ability to make changes that will accomplish this.

## Change Rating

No change here, hence no Change Rating.

## Lessons Learned

1. Any reporting relationship where the purchasing function does not report directly to the CEO reduces the potential for purchasing increasing its contribution to a company's bottom line.
2. Along those same lines, the farther purchasing is removed from reporting directly to a company's CEO increases the perception that purchasing is a tactical function whose sole deliverable is a lower purchased material pricing.
3. Unit Materials Managers are best positioned—at least with non-commodity products—to develop and design purchasing strategies and processes that best support end-use product customers, increasing market competitiveness.

# CHAPTER 4

# Nemeses

As a *change agent*, I had *up-and-down* relationships with many of my colleagues, most of whom operated *by the book* and had no interest in making significant change. When they did not agree with my proposed changes, it was not unusual for them to actively oppose them. At times, *change agents* can be regarded as rouge operators. Because of this, change proposals may result in ongoing hostility that, without support from other executives, will likely lead to being replaced or fired.

There were four such individuals with some level of control over me that made my work both difficult and risky. Below, I will generically lay out—in no particular order—the operational characteristics of the four.

## Irish

Irish was a long-time company employee who was promoted into my Division as VP of Manufacturing. This was at a time when I had about 4 years before I would qualify for retirement, with 30 years of service being the threshold for getting (a much-reduced) pension. With my employer, if a person was terminated before that time, both health insurance and stock options were lost. I had enough options that to lose them would have a significant negative financial impact, especially in regard to retirement. Because of this, it was paramount to me and my wife's financial future that I stay employed for (at least) 4 more years.

I enjoyed my job within the company and had always been a high performer. At the time, I hadn't considered leaving the company before standard retirement age, which was about 14 years away.

That all changed when Irish came into the Division. I had heard stories about how the new VP operated at other factories, none of them good. It seemed after he was moved to a new location, he left behind a trail of ruined careers while, at the same time, leaving a mess that his replacement would have to clean up.

My own first experience with Irish was at a weekly Unit staff meeting where he introduced himself and then made the following statement.

*If you're not with me, you're against me.*

That didn't sound very good to one who considered himself a *change agent* or, for that matter, anyone else on the Unit's General Manager's staff. Irish will come up in several of this book's stories. Although in one of the following chapters I will relate one instance in which Irish tried to fire me, I will not relate about the three other times he attempted to do so.

In my view, Irish had been promoted into a job that was outside the limits of his capabilities. I concluded that Irish recognized this and acted in ways in an attempt hide this, primarily by managing in a dictatorial, bullying manner.

## Imposter

The company I worked for had never had a Chief Procurement Officer. This changed when it hired an executive from another company who was recognized industry-wide for his progressive and effective approach to managing suppliers. At the time he was hired, I was an independent Materials Manager at one of the company's largest factories. In general, I was excited that the purchasing function was receiving increased corporate consideration, that is, would have a *seat-at-the-table* in enterprise strategic planning.

In our introduction to him, he confirmed that he believed in win-win collaborative management of suppliers. It turned out this was not true, at least within the framework he tried to erect at our company. Instead, he was all about gaining leverage to improve prospects in win-lose supplier negotiations in which, of course, he wanted us to be the winner and the supplier the loser. In other words, despite what he preached about progressive supply management, he was a win-lose *one-trick pony*.

While he tried to position himself as a *good guy*, he brought in an employee from his former employer that he used as a *hit-man*. In other words, he had someone he could use—applying any means necessary—to get Unit purchasing organizations to *toe-the-line* relative to corporate mandates and initiatives.

Based on the above, I considered him an *Imposter* of the worst kind.

## Darth

Many of my peers—and I—referred to the Imposter's *hit-man* as Darth. Why? When he walked into a meeting it was almost as if people sucked in their breaths in anticipation of a coming *directive*, like the reaction from his subordinates when in Star Wars, Darth Vader would enter a room filled with his subordinates. Another way of saying this is that he was a bully. I found the most effective way to deal with Darth was to stand up to him. Unfortunately, many of my peers throughout the company did not. Darth will play a role in several stories detailed in this book.

## Short-Shrift

CFOs are, in my opinion, separated from the actual factory—and supply chain—physics of running an organization. In other words, they don't really understand—or even care—about the mechanics of how things are made. Instead, they sit at their desks, look at financial documents, and set—or, at a minimum, must approve—performance goals for other operational functions without a care about whether those goals are realistic or how they are met.

For instance, I once heard a conversation between a Divisional CFO and a factory manager who was looking for suggestions on how to meet the financial goal that had been set for him. The CFO looked at him almost with distain and said "cut the number of 'shoes'." Comparing employees to footwear may be an appropriate comparison in this sense since CFO's first reaction to cutting costs was to *trod* on employees. But otherwise, it isn't.

What CFOs are really interested in doing is delivering short-term profitability to a balance sheet so they can impress stock analysts and increase company stock prices, which, in my mind, shouldn't be the sole driving issue in running a business.

# PART 2

# As a Quality Engineer

# CHAPTER 5

# A Mentor's Impact

In the introduction to this book I referred to the availability of *mentors* as an important factor for ongoing enterprise success. Luckily, I ended up with a top-notch mentor who—in reporting to him—changed both my approach to work and increased my job satisfaction. Remember this was in the mid-1980s when mentorship was encouraged, and mentors were available. As I also pointed out in the introduction to this book, mentor relationships seem to be out of fashion in today's corporate America.

The initial factory I was assigned to at my first employer was very hierarchical. Along with other restrictions, this meant that decisions—on just about everything—required managerial approval, particularly suggestions to change current strategies and processes. Another way of putting this was that at this facility, jobs had established processes that were expected to be followed step-by-step.

Consequently, during my first 7 years of employment I was allowed to make virtually no proposals or decisions relative to change. I had previously mentioned in the introduction to this book that I was primarily interested in having a career as a *change agent*. Due to my experience at this factory, I assumed that all factories at this company operated in the same manner. Because of this I started to look for a job at another employer who had a reputation of a culture that understood the value of change.

## A New Culture

At about this same time I was offered and accepted a promotion at another of my employer's factories, changing from being a Reliability Engineer to a Quality Engineer. As stated above, I assumed that this new factory would operate much like the factory I had previously worked at. Consequently, at this new location, I continued to operate similarly to how I had previously.

My new boss had weekly updates with each individual employee. I came to these meetings with proposals to increase Unit competitiveness that I would proceed with, if given approval. After laying them out, I never received sanction to proceed. In fact, he made very little comment on my ideas. This aligned, I thought, with the hierarchical culture of that previous factory I had worked at.

After a few weeks of proposing changes at my weekly updates I could see a bit of frustration on my boss's face as I walked into his office. He opened the meeting by asking me what I had accomplished since transferring to the factory. I was a bit flustered by the comment and answered that at our weekly updates I had made several proposals but had never received approval to proceed.

He frowned at this and replied:

*Paul, I'm not really interested in what you propose to do. I'm primarily interested in what* you've accomplished.

My mouth almost dropped open. As laid out above, at my previous factory, lower-level employees were required to get managerial permission to proceed with virtually any change proposal. Here, I was being told to make changes and report back on whether they had improved operational efficiency. Wow! This changed my whole approach to work, resulting in the beginning of my transformation to that of *change agent*.

Realizing that I was now working in a culture that appreciated change proposals and valued those that were successful, I dropped my job search!

## A New Work Perspective

I started to justify and implement revisions to Quality Engineering strategies and processes, two of which touched upon the purchasing function and are described in the following two chapters. You'll see that they were wildly successful in reducing cost and streamlining operations, both internally and at suppliers; which is win-win!

Probably, because of these results, a few years later I was moved to a Technical Buyer position in purchasing, where I continued justifying and implementing change. This eventually led me to being named Materials Manager.

# Summary

My experience with my first employer was very unsatisfying, both personally and professionally. This was because it was hierarchical and did not have a culture that valued or encouraged independent actions, including making change.

Because of this I started looking for a new employer. About that same time, I was transferred to another of my employer's factories that did have a culture that valued change and was lucky enough to develop a mentor–mentee relationship with my new boss that fostered my efforts at becoming a *change agent*.

# Change Rating

*Revolutionary*, both from a personal and an overall business perspective.

# Lessons Learned

- *Change agents* can deliver more value to an organization than many managers and executives appreciate.
- If an employee's primary motivation and fulfillment are satisfied without looking at ways to improve operations, they are primarily working for a paycheck.
- If you want to be a *change agent* and do not see a path toward this at your current employer, look for an employer that encourages change.
- At the end of a career, and life, for that matter, I suspect that the impacts of the changes you've made will give you the most satisfaction.

# CHAPTER 6

# Supplier Audits

Prior to my initial assignment in purchasing, I held two jobs in Quality Engineering. In the second, I had responsibility for setting up and conducting supplier audits, both in *prospecting* for new suppliers and in *assessing* current supplier capability. Although the quality function was not in either the Unit or corporate purchasing hierarchy, it was generally accepted that Quality Engineering would organize and oversee supplier audits. Their primary focus, after all, was on evaluating supplier processing capability—the bread-and-butter of manufacturing.

## The Audit Process

The scope of these audits, however, went beyond quality, including evaluation of just about every aspect of supplier operations. Audit teams were usually made up of 6 to 10 individuals.

The scheduling of audits wasn't easy. The biggest issue was getting the specialized manpower needed to be able to conduct them. It represented a several-day commitment from people from different functional areas. To say the least, this was not an easy task.

The following discussion will focus on audits of current suppliers.

## From a Supplier's Perspective

I also came to understand that a supplier's audit preparation required a significant investment in both in time and resources, and that they often took a week or more to prepare, which involved most of their entire operational team. This usually led to significant overtime expenditure and extra effort, since such preparations were required on top of the normal activities needed to getting the product out of the door.

Remember, this was before I worked in purchasing; hence, I was interested in understanding why suppliers felt they had to put this type of effort into preparing for audits. The answer I generally got when asking this question was along the lines of how an unfavorable overall assessment could lead to either significant remedial work or a loss in business or both.

From my perspective, there seemed something was wrong with the whole audit process. From a tactical point of view, audits pulled Unit people out of their normal work, putting them into roles they weren't really trained for. I was also concerned that during these audits we were observing *show-cased*—rather than normal—operations.

Finally, I wondered whether what seemed to be an excessive resource commitment by both supplier and customer delivered a meaningful return. In other words, were audits a good investment?

## An Unexpected Problem

One morning as I came into work and as I sat down at my desk, I noticed my phone flashing, indicating I had messages. Before I could review them, I got a panicked call from production telling me that an assembly line *was down* due to the leaking of a purchased component, that is, a hydraulic motor.

This supplier of the part had been audited several months ago and passed with flying colors. They had also recently received certification from a well-respected third party. It appeared from the supplier's initial feedback was that it would take a minimum of 2 weeks for them to determine and address the problem's root cause such that they could restart production and resume supply of their product to our factory. This was occurring during our factory's peak production period, and so every day of downtime represented a significant production loss and lack of machines to sell, that is, less revenue and profits.

My boss told me I had 3 days to solve the problem so that the assembly line could resume production. He went on to say that "Obviously, your supplier audits don't mean shi*, do they?"

## Determining Root Cause

My next 2 days were a whir onsite at the supplier as I reviewed their quality control program of the impacted component. The component in question had been originally developed in conjunction with us but was now an off-the-shelf product sold to other customers. As is often the case with hydraulic assemblies, there was a test fixture at the end of the assembly line that was to be used to verify all product functions, confirm pressure capabilities, and identify any fluid leakage. This test fixture had originally been sized and installed to support 100 percent of the components purchased by our factory.

Something didn't seem right. Why wasn't the final run-in detecting the leaks was carried out? The Manufacturing Manager's answer was that our assembled units were only tested periodically since the testing of each individual component would require additional test stands. The intent to not test all of our components hadn't been pointed out during the recent audit. Something didn't add up.

To say I was stunned was an understatement. Why had they made the change, and further, why hadn't they informed us of their intent to do so?

I asked why 100 percent of the assemblies weren't run through the final test stand, and I was further stunned—and upset—by his answer. After all, we had agreed to pay for the test stand in our pricing and should have been told if they were looking to revise contract terms. He told me that they had recently obtained new customers for the product and that the test stand now had to also be used to test their products.

The test stand had been sized for the volumes we needed to support our factory's production. Now what if the test stand was also being used to test assemblies of other customers, likely including some of our competitors, who weren't requiring 100 percent testing of the assemblies they'd be buying?

In addition, he said if they started testing 100 percent of our units, they would have to increase our price in order to finance additional test stands! I reminded him that their quoted price to us had specifically stated 100 percent of the units sold to our factory would be tested.

My supplier contact knew that I had him in a box and so agreed to test 100 percent of the units produced for our factory, but he would have to have to get approval from his factory's General Management.

Though we hadn't identified the root cause of the leakage, we hadn't needed to since only the ones that passed the test would be shipped to my factory. I was okay with the result!

## A Weight Lifted

The supplier's General Manager—whom I was very familiar with due to the recently completed supplier audit—sat me down to discuss the situation. I started by asking him if their final run-in test was foolproof, and he confirmed his employee's previous assertion that it was as close to being so as possible.

I next told him that from this point on all units intended for our use would be required to go through the final run-in process. He responded that since they would need to purchase additional test fixtures their additional investment would have to be reflected in a price increase. I then pointed out to him that it only seemed right that the price their additional capital cost should be covered by the new customers that were currently being run across *our* test stand.

He wasn't very happy, to say the least. I suspected this would affect the price that had been quoted to the new customers.

Seeing this, I tried to find some middle ground. I asked him how much he had spent in preparing for our recent supplier audit and what that meant relative to piece-price, assuming our current projected annual usage. He estimated that the manpower and other costs associated with preparing for and hosting it exceeded what he would need to add to our current price to increase testing capacity.

Even though I didn't really have the authority to negotiate pricing with suppliers—it was a corporate policy—I bargained with the General Manager saying that if our price remained as in the contract we would no longer audit his factory. I added that I wouldn't even tell my purchasing group about the deal we had just made!

He smiled and we shook hands on it.

## Further Savings

When I returned to my factory, I was congratulated in restarting production in 2 days. When asked if I expected any future quality problems I replied, "no," saying that we had found the reason for the leaks and corrected it—not quite the truth.

However, I still felt uncomfortable with the entire current supplier audit system. After all, if a supplier had been approved up front and was required to notify us prior to making any manufacturing change, what was the value proposition of an audit? Based on this, I unilaterally made the decision that our factory would no longer audit current suppliers.

I knew that unilaterally making this change was akin to putting my neck on the *chopping block* should an assembly line have to stop production due to a current supplier quality problem. But I had a strong enough belief that this wouldn't happen that I felt relatively comfortable instituting the change.

I did have concerns about the reaction I would receive from my colleagues in corporate quality control when I told them that our Unit was eliminating audits of prequalified current suppliers. When I explained what we were doing, I was told that such audits were a requirement and, if I had a problem with that, they would push the issue up the ladder. I told them to go ahead as I was sure over time that the data would show that eliminating the audits wouldn't negatively affect production.

Corporate did push it up the ladder, but my Unit's General Manager provided strong backing to my decision and we were able to proceed with the change. After that, I was treated as a rogue operator by corporate, as I suspected I would be. But, in the end, I had ended up doing the *right thing* for our factory and Division and so could rest easy.

Data collected over the next couple of years confirmed the decision had been a good one as we saw that neither supplier quality nor delivery performance degraded at our Unit.

It was interesting to see that during that same time period other Units across the company stopped auditing current suppliers. Eventually, this led to a corporate-wide policy, freeing up Unit resources and corporate quality resources that could be used in other areas.

## Summary

Purchasing was spending time and money conducting a non–value-added activity, that is, the auditing of current suppliers. The audits were found to not positively affect our own internal production schedules and had also led to additional supplier costs. In this instance, a *doing-the-right-thing* change—eliminating the audits—seemed to be pretty much a no-brainer.

# Change Rating

*Revolutionary*, since a cost non–value-added process was eliminated.

# Lessons Learned

- It's ok to stick your neck out if you strongly believe you have a successful solution to a current problem. In this case, both supplier and our own costs were reduced and manpower was freed up.
- It is not uncommon for there to be resistance to change by those whose jobs and responsibilities would be negatively impacted (from their perspective, anyway) by the change. It's best to anticipate this and ensure you have support from an executive sponsor.
- Finding middle ground can facilitate acceptance of a change proposal.

# CHAPTER 7

# Inspection Overload

One of my early assignments was supervising Layout Inspection. This function involved measuring parts produced by new and revised tooling to confirm that the tools and presses (let's assume we're talking about stampings)—in combination—would produce parts-to-spec on an ongoing basis. This required measuring and calculating statistical verification that part features important to fit, function, reliability and safety would be consistently met. Once a tool and the presses it would be used on were approved for production, only the first piece of every subsequent lot would need to be inspected and confirmed to be in-spec to get production approval.

Our factory included a large stamping facility; consequently, the approval of stamping tools made up a large portion of our work. At that time, we were also outsourcing a fair amount of our overall stamping requirements. One day, while walking through Receiving Inspection, I noticed an incoming lot of purchased stampings being inspected as a condition of their being released to production. In talking to the inspector, I learned that every shipment of stampings had designated specifications that—for a sample of parts—had to be verified to be in-spec for the lot to be released for production. This required significant time and effort, to the point that our factory required a workforce of over two dozen Receiving Inspectors working over three shifts to inspect incoming purchased parts.

I was also told that Quality Engineers needed to put together inspection plans to detail which critical features need to be checked on each of those inspected parts and that this took up a significant portion of each of the workload of three Quality Engineers.

# The Disconnect

I'm no genius, but it didn't take one to realize there was an inconsistency here. Specifically, our production approval process for internal stampings was different than that that we required for purchased stampings. I pointed this out to our factory's purchasing manager and made a proposal that all external stamping suppliers be required to follow our internal process—in other words, verify process capability rather than requiring their and our inspection of each outgoing/incoming lot.

He was at first dubious, but, when I pointed out the potential savings, he ended up agreeing to use stampings as a test case. I responded that that would a good sample size—we had six stamping suppliers—for a *Proof-of-Concept pilot.*

# The Change

At the time, we required that supplier part processing be approved for shipment through their inspection of all features on a sample of parts from each batch. This inspection was for all of those specifications, not just for those deemed critical. Any out-of-spec feature on any part of the inspected sample would result in the supplier having to run another batch. If none were found, the batch was approved for shipment. So, in addition to our own Receiving Inspection costs, the supplier had its own shipping approval costs.

In my pitch to our suppliers, I laid out the process we used in-house to approve our tool/press combinations and all parts subsequently manufactured using them. I explained that after proving process capability, only the first piece would have to be found in-spec for them to gain shipping approval. They understood that this would allow them to change from current resource-intensive process to a more streamlined, less costly one. And to boot, the change to assessing process capability would deliver significantly higher quality than would be possible with using the current inspection routine.

We taught these suppliers how to conduct capability studies, including calculation of CpK values and the creation of X-Bar and R Charts for every critical feature. We then confirmed that they had the measurement capability to measure the types of features and tolerances normally found on our stampings. Finally, we implemented receiving purchased stamped parts through this new framework.

## The Results

Quality improved (we compared *before* and *after* supplier quality performance), and the inspection savings were significant, both for us and our stamping suppliers. Changing the approach to both suppliers getting shipping release approval and Receiving Inspection approval for production use reduced costs significantly.

Over the next 2 years, the change was implemented with suppliers that provided the 20 percent of the parts that made up 80 percent of our incoming purchased part work. Over that period, the number of our inspectors working there was reduced to the single digits. Where were the other savings?

- Elimination of the need for Quality Engineers to create Receiving Inspection plans
- Reduction in reject resolution, that is, sorting, reworking, or shipping back to the supplier
- Reduction in production downtime
- Reduction in supplier cost.

All the above internal costs were financial exhibits that were already tracked and quantified, giving visibility to executive management of both the change and its impact.

## Getting Credit for Cutting Costs

It was important to get purchasing the credit for the internal cost savings. My satisfaction came from seeing one of my change proposals implemented. You may ask why I didn't work to get the Quality team the credit for the savings. As far as I was concerned, the most important thing was for our Unit to benefit.

At the time, Ronald Reagan was the U.S. President and he had a quote that I greatly admired:

*It's amazing what can be accomplished when people aren't concerned about who gets the credit.*

Besides, I knew that eventually people would come to understand the Quality department would be associated with the change.

## Summary

I had noticed a large discrepancy between how internal and supplier quality activities were conducted. In looking at this further, I discovered that the requirements we placed on suppliers to get shipping approval were neither statistically sound nor cost effective. I also found that significant savings would result in getting suppliers to apply our quality process to the parts we purchased from them. This change delivered significant financial results.

## Change Rating

*Revolutionary.* Although the revised processes evolved from existing practice, the overall strategy of ensuring suppliers had the capability to assure—and became responsible for—the quality of the parts supplied to our factory was a totally new approach.

## Lessons Learned

- Don't only look for change opportunities within your own functional department or even in your own plant. Processes that span several functional areas are usually ripe for improvement.
- Selling change to suppliers is easier if suppliers don't view a proposed change as *do as I say, not as I do* but see you applying the same practices.
- Recognize that superfluous supplier costs are often in place due to customer requirements. Requirements imposed on suppliers should be evaluated at least yearly to verify that they remain relevant.

# As a Technical Buyer

# CHAPTER 8

# A Basic Truth

I took my first purchasing job in 1988 as a Technical Buyer of hydraulic components. One of the responsibilities of that job was to negotiate pricing on newly designed and/or revised parts. Having only a mechanical engineering degree and experience in design, reliability, and quality, I was ill-equipped to conduct commercial negotiations. Because of this, my manager sent me to one of those *2-day-wonder* negotiating seminars You know the type, the ones that tout things like *"you don't get what you deserve—you get what you negotiate,"* implying win-lose negotiation strategy.

## The Negotiation

After attending the training, I felt I was *ready to rock*. Luckily for me, one of my first negotiation sessions was with the owner of a cylinder supplier who had been around the block at least a few times with *young bucks* like me. When we had finally arrived at what looked to be a fair agreement, I pulled the *ask-for-one-more-thing* strategy and said, "We are going to need something more to finalize this deal."

## A New Perspective

He sighed, looked me straight in the eyes, and said, "Paul, *everyone's got to eat.*"

My negotiating training hadn't prepared me for such a fundamental truth. I knew I had the leverage and could get an additional reduction in price from this supplier. But even though the process I had just been trained in would have me aggressively push for this further concession, it just didn't feel right, either personally or professionally.

After a moment of contemplation, I replied, "You're right" and shook his hand on the deal. At that moment I decided to *change* my approach to working with suppliers—specifically, from the *win-lose* strategy I had learned at the seminar to one that was more win-win.

## Avoiding a Negative Impact

This cylinder supplier was considered a *strategic* supplier, implying that it was one that should be worked with in a collaborative manner. Strategic, in this case, implying that it would either be difficult or impossible, due to things such as design or processing intellectual property, finding capable alternatives, or requiring excessive resources, cost, and time to find and bring on a new supplier.

I hadn't known this prior to the negotiation and later realized that if I had continued to try to squeeze more out of this supplier, I would have taken the first step toward undermining a collaborative relationship. Specifically, I may have gotten a minimal increase in the short term but would have likely increased costs associated with working that supplier over the longer term.

Based on this initial experience, I came to understand it was usually the best strategy to establish a collaborative win-win relationship with strategic suppliers. This may seem to some reading this chapter to not be a significant change—but it was—for the late 1980s.

## Summary

Through my first supplier negotiation I learned that my preferred—and what turned out to be the most effective—approach to working with a supplier is win-win, particularly over the longer run.

## Change Rating

*Evolutionary*, due to it transforming my understanding of negotiations. It facilitated change of my own approach to supplier management from win-lose to win-win.

# Lessons Learned

- It is important for a buyer to determine the best approach for working with individual suppliers. A *cookie-cutter* approach across an entire supply-base is seldom optimal.
- Prepare carefully for negotiations. It was a major gaffe that I hadn't realized that the supplier I was negotiating with was considered *strategic* or even understood what that meant.

# CHAPTER 9

# Fighting Fire with Fire

My belief that collaboration is a more effective price reduction strategy implies I don't apply excessive leverage on suppliers. That is not always true. Why? Because there are suppliers who aren't interested in collaboration. Below are a couple of rules I have when people—or suppliers—attempt to leverage me.

- Strategic suppliers only get one *gimme* relative to leverage and collaboration. After two instances of trying to leverage me, I will no longer work with them in a collaborative manner.
- There are instances when the tactics an outside party uses in attempting to leverage me are so obnoxious that I work to gain leverage and apply it harshly on them.

## A Bad Day to Be a Buyer

Hearing that one of your suppliers has filed for bankruptcy can be like walking into your office and seeing a film crew from *60 Minutes* waiting for you. This is something a purchasing professional never wants to be associated with.

You might think that a bankruptcy should never be a surprise to a vigilant buyer. With public companies this is usually true, since they are required to issue periodic reports that provide a clear window into their financial health. This type of transparency is not, however, generally available for companies that are privately held.

## Being Leveraged

I once received a call from a lawyer representing a bank. He said that he had been told by the owner of one of my suppliers that I was their contact within my company. The lawyer went on to say that the supplier was in receivership and that his bank now owned all of its assets. I then asked if arrangements could be made to retrieve our tooling. He responded that this was exactly the purpose of his call and that we could take possession of our tooling for $200,000! I was a bit stunned by this offer and my subsequent answer was twofold, as follows:

- The initial cost of the five tools located at that supplier had initially cost had about $44,000.
- My company and the supplier had signed tooling bailment agreements that meant that we already owned them.

The lawyer told me that he was aware of the bailment agreements but, regardless, his bank was prepared to go to court to contest our ownership claims. I knew that this threat implied we would not have the tooling for a long time, which was unacceptable. He ended our discussion by asking whether we were going to pay his bank the $200,000. I said I'd get back to him. After checking on the quantity of the bankrupt supplier's raw material we had on hand—it would only support a little over 2 weeks' worth of production—I hurried to my supervisor to ask for guidance.

## Remedial Action

His first words were, "How did you let this happen?" He went on to say that I needed to understand that it would not be acceptable for a lack of parts from one of *my* suppliers to interrupt production. When I asked what actions, he'd recommend he replied, "I'm sure you'll figure it out. Why don't you go and consult with Chuck?"

Chuck was a purchasing colleague. His persona was that of both a balladeer and pirate. I went over to Chuck and explained the situation to him. His first question was, "Where is this supplier located?" I replied they were *local*, under 2-hour drive or so from our factory.

He then asked whether I might know of a door we could use to enter their building. My answer here was "yes" because I was aware of a backdoor my supplier contact used to go out in the afternoons when he wanted to get an early start on a round of golf!

Finally, he asked if I knew where our tooling was stored in the supplier's factory. I said I did since I visited my local suppliers regularly and, as a result, had a pretty good handle on where they were stored.

Chuck then said, "Come over to my house after dinner and we'll go take care of business."

## Taking the Bull (Tools) by the Horns

I rolled up to Chuck's house just as the sun was going down, and he told me what our *mission* was. He explained to me that we were going retrieve what was ours, that is, the tooling. I told him I was confused by this explanation because I knew the shop would be closed and there would be no-one around. He just smiled.

When we got to the supplier we drove directly to the "golfing exit" door and found it unlocked. We then went into the building and located our tooling. The tools themselves weighed only a little over 100 pounds each so, with a little muscle power, we were able to lift them onto an available shop cart and then wheel them out and load them in the bed of Chuck's truck.

The next day I took Chuck's truck with the tools to another local supplier that produced parts from the same product grouping as the one who had just gone into receivership. He smiled when he saw me and what I had brought, immediately understanding *what was up*; that is, I'm sure he had heard on the grapevine of his competitor's bankruptcy. He looked over the tools and said there would be no problem fitting them up to his equipment. I immediately gave him a verbal purchase order, and, within 2 weeks, he had qualified his processes and was shipping parts to us.

## Calling the Bluff

I then went back to the office and called the bank's lawyer. He asked if my company had decided to go ahead and pay the $200,000 in order to access the tooling. I admit that I lied to him. I told him that, unbeknownst to me, I had found out that the tooling fabricator that we had originally bought the tools from always built two sets, in case a customer broke or wore out a tool and needed an immediate replacement. And so, in this case, we had purchased the duplicate tools from him for the original cost, that is, $44,000.

I then said, "Keep the tools—they were getting worn anyway." The lawyer was silent for a minute and then asked what he was supposed to do with them. I suggested his bank sell them for scrap and he ended the conversation by saying—"You know, that $200,000 price was just a starting point—we would have settled for $44,000." I replied that he should be more upfront with the next company that he was trying to steal from and hung up.

## Summary

The above event occurred in the late 1980s, before the availability of inexpensive security cameras or cellphones with cameras. I knew the supplier in question didn't use security guards and suspected the bank wouldn't use them either. We never heard back from the bank, so I suspect they never figured out that our tools were missing.

## Change Rating

*Evolutionary*, since we were able to keep our assembly line from being shut down, which meant we would have enough product to meet expected demand. It also showed that you don't have to operate under unethical parameters set by someone else; that is, you can impose your own set of rules.

## Lessons Learned

- Don't allow yourself or your company to be bullied. Find ways to change and/or reverse the leveraging factors.
- There is usually more than one way to get out of a negative situation. In this case, it was more or less to *fight fire with fire*.
- Spending time onsite with suppliers can result in unexpected benefits.

# CHAPTER 10

# When Costs Go Down, Prices Go Down

At my first job in purchasing my responsibilities included prospecting for new suppliers: making sourcing decisions and connecting suppliers with our engineers to develop spec and design changes that would allow for lower processing costs. In this job, my span of responsibility included, among other things, hydraulic components.

One of the first things I did was put together a Pareto analysis of the spend I had responsibility for, identifying those parts that had the most cost-reduction potential, based on previous year-to-year price increases. After identifying them, I did find that one of the hydraulic components I purchased—a steering valve—stood out.

## The Component's Background

One of the parts in question was a hydraulic steering valve that was used on one of our higher-priced SKUs (Stock Keeping Units). I found that over the previous 5 years it had increased in price by over 30 percent! This was during the 1980s—so inflation was a factor—but the price increases on this part were way above anything else in my buy.

I called the supplier in question to have them explain the basis for their price increases and really didn't get much of an answer. They did, however, let me know that the increase for the upcoming year looked to be in the 7 to 8 percent range!

After the call, I investigated the availability of alternate sources and found that none currently existed. This helped me understand that the supplier of this component felt it had all of the leverage and wasn't shy about exerting it.

The source issue wasn't whether there were other suppliers of hydraulic steering valves. There were. Our use of this type of this component was, however, a bit unique in that it operated at a significantly lower hydraulic pressure relative to the applications of their other customers. In other words, alternate supplier product designs and processing were targeted for applications requiring the much tighter tolerances needed to support higher-pressure systems.

The current supplier had gotten our business by coming up with an alternative approach to housing design and fabrication that, I'll admit, was innovative and out-of-the-box. Rather than machining castings for the assembly housing, they manufactured theirs by fabricating tight-tolerance stamped plates and then bolting them together. Their specialized stamping process could not hold the tight tolerances achievable only with machining but were good enough for the lower pressures needed for our application.

I then found out there was one other, but important, consideration, relative to a potential sourcing change. My employer owned an assembly plant in the same small town as the current source of the steering valves. The manager of our facility was against any resourcing from them *unless there was a significant justification*. Why? The supplier employed the larger part of the workers in the town, and, should we resource from them, it was likely that he would become persona non grata there.

## Changing the Balance of Leverage

In my search for alternate sources, I found a supplier that other company Divisions had successfully worked with in a collaborative way. I approached this supplier, and we brainstormed about how we might significantly reduce the cost of one of their current product offerings without *reinventing the wheel*. In other words, they were open to considering tweaks to their current design and processing but were not willing to take a greenfield approach since our business alone would not represent enough volume to justify their investing in development of a new product.

It turned out that their current housing processing included three sequential machining steps, with each successive one used to tighten the tolerances needed by the bulk of their other customers. Each different step required post-process inspection as well as setup on a succeeding machine.

I asked if they could adjust their initial rough machining operation such that it alone could provide the tolerances needed to support our lower-system-pressure operations and, in doing so, eliminate the need for second and third machining operations. They said they'd look into it and, a week or two later, got back to me. My contact was excited to tell me their manufacturing engineers had confirmed that with minimal adjustment, the first rough machining operation would suffice. We then mocked up a couple of prototypes and tested them, both in the lab and on operational equipment. They performed just fine.

The next step was to cost-out the steering valve based on the revised processing. Based on our calculations, I gave them a *target cost*—based on cost management analysis—and they came relatively close to meeting it. I then asked if they would agree to a several-year contract relative to controlling prices, that is, where we would only honor non-controllable pricing impacts such as those for material.

They got together with their accountants and executive management and accepted these terms. As far as I was concerned, we could start the process of resourcing the assembly and capture a huge price reduction.

## The Go-Ahead

Aside the foregoing activities discussed, I knew I wouldn't be the one to make the final decision on the resourcing since it was considered a critical component. Our next step involved putting together a proposal to upper management—Engineering, Purchasing, and other Divisional executives—to get their blessing. In other words, we needed to financially justify the change. I suspected that supplier participation in the presentation would make it easier to get the go-ahead since they would be better positioned to answer any technical questions that came up. So, I asked my contact from the supplier to co-present at the decision meeting.

The presentation went well and afterward I got approval to resource to the cost-reduced component which led to my first, annualized seven-figure savings. The bottom line here was that my employer got a significant price reduction on an expensive component. The supplier and I accomplished this by adjusting the part's processing to better align with our application's needs. This allowed both a cost/price reduction and also resulted in our new source taking a pretty big chunk of new business from a prime competitor and at the same time creating a new revenue stream. This was certainly a win-win collaboration.

When the incumbent supplier learned they were losing the business they immediately offered a 33 percent price reduction. In turning them down, I replied that it wasn't just a matter of price. Rather, it was that my company wanted to work with suppliers who wouldn't leverage us at the first opportunity, and, regarding this point, they had lost our trust.

Over a 5-year term the incumbent supplier had enjoyed a financial benefit. However, after that, they lost all of their low-pressure steering valve business and, as a consequence, had to close their factory and lose all of the investment they had made in setting it up.

## Summary

A supplier of a hydraulic component had been raising their price above the norm for several years. They were able to do this since they had no competition in the functional needs of our product. By working collaboratively with another hydraulic component manufacturer, we were able to take one of their higher performance steering valves and revise its processing to both meeting our products needs and sell it to us and a significant—far into the double figures—cost reduction. The reduction, in fact, resulted in a much-reduced price on a part with which we had been paying another supplier over 5 years.

The incumbent supplier had taken advantage of us for shorter-term profitability that eventually led to a catastrophic blow to their overall business.

## Change Rating

*Revolutionary*, since it showed that significant savings can result due to changes resulting from collaboration with a supplier in their development of a new product offering that delivered their customer a significant price break.

# Lessons Learned

- Prices go down when costs go down. Developing collaborative working relationships with strategic suppliers is an effective approach to win-win cost reductions.
- Identifying supply-base price-increase *outliers* is a good approach to recognize the cost-reduction potential of the purchased products.
- Having a sole source for a product without a Plan B, that is, alternate supplier or long-term contract, should be regarded as a *red flag* for future problems.
- You owe little or no loyalty to suppliers who try to take advantage of you.

# CHAPTER 11

# The Case for Supplier Development

There is, and has always been, the question of whether or not a purchasing department should devote resources to assist incumbent suppliers increase their competitiveness—those that elect to staff up and offer assistance—primarily industrial engineering support—to reduce supplier cost. Although this is generally the stated supplier development goal, several different approaches were developed, some of which were win-win, others not so much.

An OEM I once worked for had—at its height—dedicated a couple of dozen resources to supplier development. Another I worked at committed already existing internal functional resources to assist suppliers in their area of expertise.

## Prevailing Thought

Today—where OEMs still do designate resources to supplier development—there seems to be less of a focus on a win-win strategy. So, what has happened?

This is not difficult to understand. Remember, in the 1990s, the concept of supplier development had to go up against a tidal wave of sourcing to low-price countries. I remember very vividly—as a newly minted Manager of Strategic Sourcing I had been charged with starting up a supplier development function within my Division and presenting my plans for this to a group of executives. As it happened, a couple of Brooks Brothers–clad consultants were in attendance that day. They had, in fact, been hired to evaluate our Division's purchasing strategies and practices.

One of these *suits* interrupted me shortly into my presentation saying he had never heard *anything so ridiculous* (his words). He went on to say there was really no need to expend resources for developing incumbent domestic suppliers when lower prices were readily available in China or India. I didn't even get to finish my presentation.

Fortunately, after the meeting, one of the Division's top executives told me to continue on with the supplier development initiative I was proposing, which is referred to in several chapters of this book.

## A Small Rodent Strategy

Unfortunately, large corporations heeded the call to source overseas in almost a *lemming-like* manner, deciding that negotiating lower piece-prices was the primary goal of purchasing. They believed they could best be obtained by sourcing to low-price (note, not necessarily lowest total cost) countries. I believed—and still do—that the overriding goal of purchasing should be the development of a World-Class Supply-Base. As discussed above, most procurement executives of my generation translated that to a singular goal of lowering the cost of purchased material, to the exclusion of all other factors. I don't think that too many companies today would argue that the overseas sourcing phenomena hasn't yielded World-Class performance from their suppliers, which got increased visibility during the COVID-19 pandemic.

For instance, overseas sources have inherently lengthy *true* lead-times. OEMs found that building to demand—or otherwise changing schedules on short notice—exposed them to order fulfillment difficulties. Logistics-related *true* lead-times from overseas suppliers are on the order of 4 to 6 weeks. Added to that, I've seen plenty of contracts with overseas sources that required a *90-days-firm* schedule commitment. In that case, adding 3 months to the time needed to account for transportation results in a supplier response time of 4 to 6 months.

Needless to say, *true* lead-times of this magnitude cannot support the short-fuse schedule changes needed to respond to market demand that varies from forecast. The only way to address the accompanying order fulfillment issue is to have prebuilt purchased part inventory on hand, which, of course, implies anything but World-Class. It also means that parts may be over- or under-stocked, which can lead to either a loss of sales or carry-over inventory.

So perhaps win-win supplier development deserves another look as a vehicle for achieving that World-Class Supply-Base goal. But let's first look at the goal most companies put in front of their supplier development function.

## Supplier Order Fulfillment Crises

When a supplier cannot support orders due to quality problems, lack of capacity, and so on, that negatively affects an OEM's production schedule, it is typically referred to as a *drop-everything-event*. In these instances, supplier development resources are usually 100 percent tasked with helping the supplier in question get into a position where they *can* support their customer production schedule. In other words, supplier development takes on the role of a firefighter—which is tactical, not strategic.

It is difficult to argue against the need of firefighting, but (hopefully) it isn't a frequent need in the big-picture scheme of supply chain performance.

## Supplier Price Reduction Shortfalls

Many OEMs have annual price reduction expectations. When suppliers don't meet them, they may offer them supplier development assistance to aid in improving their operational efficiency with an eye toward cost reduction. One role supplier development is given *is to find ways a supplier can reduce price soon after engagement*. I won't argue with this role, but I know first-hand that it puts the supplier development function in the position of needing to look for quick-hit improvements rather than sustainable fixes that will improve a supplier's ongoing effectiveness over the long haul.

Fundamental improvements require intensive support, and waste elimination in processes, and it normally takes longer to identify and address areas of waste. But at the same time, it is also true that they can have the effect of delivering larger and ongoing cost/price reductions.

Why *ongoing*? Because as part of a supplier development team suppliers are taught through project activities to *learn-how-to-fish*, such that they have a defined process going forward for continuing waste elimination on their own.

I'll add that an OEM focused on short-term price reduction is typically looked upon as anything but *benevolent* by suppliers. In this case, more often than not, they see supplier development–type support as a way for their customer to learn the ins and outs of their cost drivers, with a goal of understanding and cutting supplier margins. At least this is how suppliers I have talked to see it.

Because of this, it soon became clear that there were supplier concerns related to supplier development resources learning information that could be used as leverage in win-lose negotiations.

To address this issue, our supplier development engagements were structured around a Memorandum of Understanding (MOU), which specifically stated that the supplier o*wns all their internal operational data* and that data could only be shared with internal OEM personnel with approval by the supplier.

## What Should the Supplier Development Role Be?

Supplier development should have the role of assuring that *strategic* suppliers are working their way toward becoming World-Class. In other words, the function should play an integral role of developing Lean suppliers rather than aimed at delivering short-term financial gains. As discussed elsewhere in this book, *true* lead-time reduction should be used as a primary strategy for assisting suppliers to achieve a World-Class status.

Being World-Class isn't part of any supplier performance evaluation that I know of.

## Summary

Every functional area must change to maintain its competitiveness. Unfortunately, one such area that has not changed primary strategies and process since the dawn of America's *industrial revolution* is purchasing. If you don't agree with this, ask yourself if you really think your approach to purchasing varies much from that used by Henry Ford—mainly win-lose negotiations—to get lower pricing.

This means that though manufacturing has transitioned from buying commodities—so they could fabricate most of the parts/assemblies needed to manufacture their product internally—today most purchases are designed products that require suppliers to have specialized manufacturing process. Yet many OEMs continue to attempt to buy them as if they were commodities.

Applying Fordist strategies has not and will not produce World-Class suppliers. Collaboration seems to be the key to accomplishing this and that supplier development is a key factor in developing collaboration.

## Change Rating

*Revolutionary.* Managing strategic suppliers more as departments outside of an OEM's factory walls than independent entities represents a fundamental change in supply management strategy and practice.

## Lessons Learned

- Raising the importance of understanding the need for and setting *true* lead-time targets should be regarded as having the same importance of doing so for quality and delivery when making sourcing decisions. Having *true* lead-time alignment with customer market dynamics should be regarded as a needed metric for a supplier to be judged World-Class.
- If you can support a current initiative such as delivering shorter-term price reductions—while at the same time work on developing an alternative approach that will facilitate the supplier's endeavor toward reaching World-Class status—do so *under the radar.* This will give you the opportunity to develop *pilot* results that will justify the change you will propose. It is the rare executive who will support an Evolutionary or Revolutionary change based on a *leap-of faith*.

# CHAPTER 12

# A Supplier Development Strategy

## Increasing Market Competitiveness

The Division of our company in which I worked manufactured relatively expensive consumer products that were primarily sold either through company stores—whose business was chiefly based on large off-road commercial products—or small garage-shop types of operations—whose primary business was small engine repair.

These marketing outlets carried little else except our company's products. Hence, the volume of shoppers passing through them would be people looking to buy other products and/or services. This business model significantly limited sales.

As a solution to this problem, a decision was made to market products through the Big Box marketing channel. Big Box Stores sell many types of products, and, with consumers tending to prefer one-stop shopping, it was felt that this additional visibility would likely spur shoppers who had not previously considered our products to do so.

The overriding question, then, became what would be the change(s) needed to successfully sell through this new marketing channel and, perhaps more importantly, how do we implement them?

Big Box Stores had vastly different order fulfillment requirements than our current dealers. They require very short order fulfillment lead-times since they only carry the inventory onsite they anticipate needing to support their weekly sales. Consequently, a Big Box Stores' weekly schedule changes could require increasing the volume of specific SKUs delivered to them. It was important to support these order changes since other competitive brands were available in the store and, if your product wasn't available, customers would consider purchasing one from a competitor. On top of this, if an order was late, the Big Box Store would penalize their source by deducting from the price they paid for it.

Although our own factory was quite responsive, our supply chain didn't have the manufacturing agility to support the needed order replenishment time without reduction of *true* lead-times, and neither did our competitors. If we were not able to increase the responsiveness of our supply chain, we would have to rely on the same strategy they did by shipping from prebuilt, prepositioned finished goods inventory, a very expensive strategy.

Even though Big Box Stores sold competitive brands, we believed customers would opt to purchasing ours, for several reasons. First, our products had the highest reputation for quality and function in the industry. We also knew from testing competitive products that ours were both more reliable and had a longer life than theirs.

Consequently, we thought any risk competing with onsite competitors was worth it to gain the store foot-traffic we were looking for.

Our primary goal was to sell at a lower cost than that of our competitors. We knew that if we could reduce supplier response time, we could avoid the cost of prebuilt inventory, which would deliver higher profitability. The opportunity this presented led to it being adopted as the primary strategy of our change initiative.

## A Supply Chain Development Strategy

As stated above, our own factory had the capability to respond to short-fuse orders from customers. As Materials Manager, I had the responsibility for increasing the order fulfillment agility of strategic suppliers. The bottom line for purchasing was that our supplier development team would need to work with 80 strategic suppliers to lower their lead-times.

I had become aware of a statement from (then) Toyota's North America Chief Purchasing Officer, Simon Nagata. Specifically, Nagata had said that their strategy for selecting and working with suppliers was based on the tenet:

*Time Is the Shadow of Waste.*

That thought sure caught my attention. Based on it, I decided I needed to know more about Toyota philosophy. In doing so, I came across a quote from Taiichi Ohno, considered the father of the Toyota Production System:

*All we are doing is looking at the timeline from the moment the customer gives us an order to the point when we collect the cash. And we are reducing that time by removing the non-value-added wastes.*

Based on this, I concluded that Toyota's approach to Lean was to focus on reducing supplier *true* lead-times through waste reduction. This statement led to legitimization of our supplier development strategy, which I would use in selling it to higher management. I also realized due to Ohno's position that *true* lead-time could be used as a metric for *Leanness*, that is, waste reduction. For instance, the longer the *true* lead-time, the less Lean the manufacturer, while the shorter it was, the Leaner the manufacturer. This meant that shortening *true* lead-times also had the potential to deliver other desirable benefits.

I quickly latched on to this concept since reduction of *true* lead-times was exactly what would be needed to reduce our reliance on prebuilt finished good inventory, yet still successfully satisfy the order fulfillment policies of Big Box Stores. Supplier development engagements, then, would not be focused directly on cost/price reduction. Rather, waste elimination would be prioritized based on the potential for reducing *true* lead-time. Yet, due to this strategy, cost/price would likely go down.

## The Missing Link

I was surprised in my perusal of the Toyota Production System to find that no metric or definition for *true* lead-time was cited or even defined. Because of this we knew we would need to develop our own. *True* lead-time is what we came up with, as follows:

*The typical amount of calendar time from when a manufacturing order is created through the critical-path until the first, single end-item of that order is delivered to the customer.*

There is a lot of power in this definition, including the following salient aspects:

- It reflects *true* lead-times due to its critical-path focus, in which prebuilt/prepositioned inventories (raw, in-process, or finished product) are translated to elements of time.
- It is based on what end-use customers care about when ordering product, that is, the calendar time they must wait for a product that is not in stock.
- Delivery of a *single end-item* penalizes batches that are above and beyond current customer demand. The larger the batch size, the larger the *true* lead-time. This is because batch sizes above current demand increases the length of the critical-path.

I later came across the following story that further cemented our needed supplier development strategy:

*While being walked through the factory of a large U.S. aircraft manufacturer, Mr. (James) Womack (one of the originators of the term Lean) was shown an operation that had just undergone successful kaizen-based set-up reduction. After hearing about its impact on the process' operational metrics, he asked his guides how the work had improved overall final assembly throughput, that is, "Had the project shortened airplane (true) lead-times?" After a bit of discussion, they replied that the operation that had been worked on wasn't on the overall product's critical path, so the project hadn't impacted finished throughput. Womack replied "Then why in the world were you working on that operation!"*

*True* lead-time reduction, then, became the foundation of our supplier development strategy in working with suppliers to position them to align with the manufacturing agility needed to support our Division's entry into the Big Box marketing channel.

## Summary

A goal had been set to significantly increase sales of our Division's products, while at the same time increasing margins on those sales. It became apparent that selling product through the Big Box marketing channel—while at the same time reducing a reliance on prebuilt finished product inventory to meet their short-fuse order changes—would be required to meeting this goal.

Doing so would require a significant change in how new suppliers were selected and the development of a metric that both quantified *Leanness* and supplier order fulfillment agility. It would also require intensive onsite supplier development collaboration with incumbent suppliers to facilitate an increase in their order fulfillment agility.

## Change Rating

*Revolutionary*, in terms of using *true* lead-time reduction as a primary supplier development strategy, as well as development of a metric of Lean that seemed to fill a gap in the Toyota Production System, at least as how it was introduced to U.S. and European manufacturers.

## Lessons Learned

- There are practices that are considered *sacred cows* under the assumption that they must not be changed. One such belief in our company was that all products would only be sold through company dealers. This was seen as a barrier to increasing sales. Regardless, we understood that this would have to change to meet our goals.

  The conclusion here is not be afraid of proposing challenging sacred cows when they obstruct increasing market competitiveness.

- Our Division began to recognize our order fulfillment performance depends on having a Lean Supply-Base. Similarly, it became apparent that being able to support a product's market dynamics with minimal waste is an important capability of World-Class suppliers.

- Purchasing's representation and its input in the development of a new business strategy and the changes required to implement it led to the function having a *seat at the table*, as it was apparent that this was essential to increasing company competitiveness. In other words, purchasing should no longer be considered a tactical function.

# CHAPTER 13

# Supplier Development Is Purchasing

After a successful supplier Proof-of-Concept pilot, our Division implemented several additional successful projects at several other suppliers. Based on this, I got a call from the President of another one of the company's Divisions, which didn't have a supplier development group. He wanted a face-to-face meeting to discuss the reason that our Division did.

In our industry, it was not unusual to have supplier overlap with competitors. In other words, suppliers would sell similar products both to us and those we were competing against. I adopted a strategy of offering supplier development assistance to such suppliers. Our philosophy was that significant supplier improvement could only be achieved by implementing changes to their complete operation. Consequently, this meant that to achieve our goals, we'd have to reduce supplier's costs across their entire factory.

## Points and Counterpoints

The President's headquarters was a 5-hour drive from the factory where I worked, which meant the round-trip and meeting would take 2 full days out of my schedule. But I understood that if I were to convince other Units/Divisions to dedicate resources to the supplier development function, the trip would be necessary.

When I met with the other Division's President, he laid his main argument against allocating resources to supplier development. He said that we spend a lot of money on purchased parts. For this money, our suppliers should accept responsibility for improving their own operations. Based on this, he asked why we should allocate additional money and resources to help.

My answer was that purchasing had operated under that doctrine for decades, but doing so had not resulted in development of World-Class Supply-Bases. I went on to say that continuing with such a strategy it was unlikely to do so going forward and that this would be a barrier to both getting cost/price reductions as well as our own company being regarded as World-Class. He frowned when I made this comment.

I also pointed out that assisting strategic suppliers to improve their overall operation would likely give us a competitive advantage since it would go a long way toward establishing a collaborative relationship that would give us an advantage over our competition.

I added that if he had any other ideas to accomplish this, I would appreciate him sharing them with me.

He didn't suggest any.

Another point he made was that supplier development resources should only assist suppliers reduce processing costs on the parts they made for us.

My answer to this was three-fold. First, such an approach would not result in significant supplier cost reduction since it wouldn't fundamentally change a supplier's approach to manufacturing, leaving their overall operational costs essentially the same. Consequently, this would limit the benefits we would get out of the supplier development engagement.

Second, I doubted suppliers would tell our competitors of any savings related to the manufacture of their parts, and I knew that I wouldn't!

Third, I said that supplier development assistance would cement a collaborative relationship between our company and the supplier. Based on this, I had no doubt that going forward they would give us more favorable terms than those given to any of their other customers, including the competition.

Finally, and I could see from his face that he knew he couldn't really argue with this point, I said that even if comprehensive supplier development support resulted in the same level of price reduction to the competition, I had no doubt that on a level-playing field we could outperform anybody!

I knew he would have a difficult time taking a position counter to that argument!

But he was not done. He said he had reviewed my improvement strategy and that while it might make sense theoretically, what proof did I have that using it would reduce both our purchased material costs and improve supplier ability to support short-fuse schedule changes?

I had anticipated this question and had a ready answer. I shared the results of our three pilot projects, as follows.

## Supplier Number 1:

- *True* lead-time was reduced from 15 days to 2 days.
- Supplier On-time Delivery and As-Delivered Quality performance improved.
- The price of our parts sourced from the supplier was reduced by 11 percent.

## Supplier Number 2:

- *True* Lead-time was reduced from 32 days to 2 days.
- Both On-time Delivery and As-Delivered Quality performance improved.
- The price of the parts sourced from the supplier was reduced by 10 percent.

## Supplier Number 3:

- *True* Lead-time was reduced from 22 days to 10 days.
- Highly rated On-time Delivery and Quality performance were maintained.
- The price of the parts sourced from that supplier was reduced by 6 percent.

This pretty much was the end of the meeting. I left not really having any idea what its result would be.

Eventually, the President did give his purchasing group permission to staff internal supplier development resources. It was shortly after this that I was named Process Owner of a company-wide supplier development initiative.

# Summary

I was asked by the President of one of our corporation's other Divisions to justify my proposal that all company Units/Divisions add supplier development resources and adopt the project implementation process that our Division had demonstrated was highly effective. There was resistance to the changes I proposed but, eventually, many of them were adopted.

# Change Rating

*Revolutionary*, since all company Divisions eventually opted to dedicate purchasing resources to a supplier development function.

# Lessons Learned

- Regardless of the business plan justification and/or actual pilot results you can cite, proposing change to higher-level executives with preexisting differing views can be a hard sell. Choose your battles wisely.
- Don't be intimidated when selling a change proposal at the executive level if you can show that it has increased, and will increase, company competitiveness. Should it not be accepted, the onus will be on them for an explanation of their decision not to support it, especially if other Units/Divisions that do adopt it outperform theirs.
- Prepare for the meeting. I had anticipated the arguments he would present against my proposal, which added to my proposal presentation.
- Successfully making the case for change at the executive level can be good for a career.

# CHAPTER 14

# A Reality Check

## Background

Anyone who has been involved in a due diligence assessment of potential sources knows that to be competent at this task requires significant experience as well as time and effort on site at a supplier. In spite of this, about 25 years ago, several commercial companies started marketing *online auctions* as an alternative to the traditional sourcing process. These companies offered to take over responsibility for supplier capability assessment and then host a real-time Dutch Auction in which their potential sources would vie for business.

A Dutch Auction involves real-time bidding between potential sources until a lowest overall price is arrived at. The advertising by the firms conducting them virtually guaranteed OEMs lower purchased part pricing.

## Initial Experience

I got involved with online auctions in the late 1990s when my new boss believed that online auctions—which had not been used within our company up to that time—would prove to be an efficient lower-cost method of sourcing and/or resourcing.

To try out this approach, he told me to conduct an online auction on our *machined parts* buy. I questioned, "Why this product category?" He responded that compared to our previous in-house machining costs—most of which had been outsourced over the last several years—he felt it had great potential for reduced pricing. I pointed out to him that over the last 2 years we had provided extensive supplier development support to our sole source of machined parts and, in my opinion, they were World-Class. He just smirked and said, "Make it so."

The cost to an OEM for a Dutch Auction is for the upfront setup and preparation. What the OEM is essentially paying for is the auctioneer's promise to bring a set of capable supplier participants within the targeted commodity to compete against your incumbent source(s). For the machined parts auction, our upfront fee was (at the time in the mid-1990s) $100,000.

Putting together quote packages for a group of potential suppliers (in our case, six) that we had never previously engaged took a lot of time, effort, and cost. So, our upfront cost to the auction was more than the out-of-pocket $100,000.

The cost borne by the suppliers who win business takes the form of a never-ending manufacturer's representative fee of about 3 to 4 percent of their total won business. So, no matter who wins, the online auction company gets a significant *agency* fee.

The machined parts online auction event ended up being a *goat rodeo*, to put it diplomatically. With over a 100 part numbers *on bid*, the online auction company's alternative sources didn't get anywhere near the pricing from our current supplier. In fact, they generally came in at about 8–10 percent above them.

I was happy that my previous contention about our machining supplier being World-Class looked to be on target and was an endorsement of the effectiveness of our supplier development engagements!

The results were surprising to my boss, but he eventually agreed that perhaps we had chosen the wrong product type as a test case for the process. To that point he told me to organize another online auction, this time in a product category to which supplier development support hadn't been previously provided.

## A Second Trial

The wireform product category was selected as the focus of the next auction. I won't get into the details of wire-form processing other than to say that their manufacture is at least as much *art* as *science*. In other words, without a comprehensive knowledge of the capability of the equipment that will be used in their manufacture, it is difficult to predict up front whether actual supplier processing will consistently manufacture parts to spec. Consequently, in looking for a new source of wireforms, one of our prime considerations was whether the company had someone with significant tribal knowledge of their manufacturing processes.

It soon became apparent that our online Dutch Auction service provider hadn't included this in their evaluation and left us questioning whether they have even done a capability assessment.

Over a 100 part numbers were up for bid in this auction, too, and about two-thirds of them ended up being resourced to new suppliers.

## The Rest of the Story

My boss felt that these results were probably more than representative of the potential of the process.

Bottom line, implementation was frustration. Here's what we experienced.

By contract, we had a 90-day window with suppliers when business was to be resourced from them. In other words, our current suppliers agreed up front that if they lost business, they would continue to maintain supply of the parts in question for a period of 90 days.

Shortly into the transition of the first package it became apparent that one of the suppliers was having difficulty in producing to spec the parts they had *won* in the auction. This left us in a quandary since we needed to maintain *continuity of supply* to our production lines. As a result, I had to take a road trip to our incumbent supplier to request that they continue supplying us past the contractual 90-day window. It was apparent to me that our putting their business up for bid online had soured their opinion of us as a customer. In other words, they weren't really interested in doing any further business with us.

After much cajoling—and personnel groveling—they agreed to continue to supply us but at a 20 percent premium above our current pricing. Of course, to avoid paying this price over the long run, we worked to resource these parts, which again, took time, effort, and expense.

The other two successful bidders also had trouble consistently producing all the parts they had won to spec, and we had to return them to the incumbent suppliers. Gratefully, the other two that had lost business took the parts back without a price increase.

So, what was the result of this second auction?

1. Little overall financial benefit. It took us several months to source the parts of the 20 percent premium supplier. Luckily for us, the other two incumbent suppliers did not increase their price on the returned parts.
2. The auction company did not refund the $200,000 we had paid them to cover the two upfront setup fees, despite their failure to deliver what they had guaranteed.
3. A significant amount of purchasing and engineering resources were required in doing the required prep work for the parts that would be up for auction. This represented a significant added cost.
4. There were two additional suppliers to manage—with minimal parts—within the part category. Managing more suppliers took more time and resources and added cost.
5. The two new *successful* suppliers ended up on the lower end of our ongoing supplier performance reports.

Going back to the initial statement about evaluating potential new sources, our two experiences made it obvious that the online auctioneer wasn't up to the task.

## Summary

A new process was proposed that was piloted with two suppliers. The pilot results were extremely negative, and the process was not adopted across the organization.

## Change Rating

No change, hence, no Change Rating. But the activity did put together an indisputable Proof-of-Concept business case such that our company should have no further engagement with Dutch Auctioneers. In other words, it saved the corporation significant expense and resources.

# Lessons Learned

- Sourcing through online auctions may be value-adding for commodities, such as pens and pencils, but do not apply well to designed parts and/or assemblies.
- Choose your outside services wisely. Working with online auctioneers solidifies in some the flawed idea that purchasing is truly a tactical function.
- If a proposed change seemed too good to be true, it probably is.
- Change management should also be involved in evaluating proposed changes that, in the end, make no economic sense. In other words, helping their organization to not adopt a proposed change.

# CHAPTER 15

# Print Reviews and Feature Cost Manuals

## The Print Review Process

Our factory conducted print reviews of all newly designed purchased parts. The participants in each review included:

1. Product Engineers, who were responsible for parts' fit and function as well as safety. Industrial Engineers, who were responsible for parts on the production line, with a joint goal to both eliminate waste and to assure ease of assembly. Purchasing personnel, who were responsible for ensuring that purchasing parts were to spec and competitively priced.
2. The supplier from whom the part was to be sourced, who was responsible for ensuring that lowest-cost manufacturing processes were employed in producing part features and specifications.

All print review participants also brainstormed for a different, lower-cost design that would still meet parts' functional and safety requirements. And, of course, another important goal of print reviews was to reduce manufacturing costs to lower a part's price.

## Resource Requirement

Print reviews played an important role in the new part release process, but they were also resource-intensive. Again, at the time, they were conducted as face-to-face sessions with all participants and lasted, on average, between 2 and 3 hours. That might not seem like much, but it adds up when you're talking about dozens, or more, new parts needed on a product. Consequently, the reviews were difficult to schedule since each participant had their *day jobs* and were highly protective of their time.

Obviously, if there was a way to streamline print reviews, it would reduce the resource commitment from the various functional areas.

At the time, print reviews were just gaining popularity at progressive OEMs. In our experience, they were quite effective, most delivering cost reductions, sometimes in the double digits.

Each session reviewed part features and specifications to ensure that they were properly toleranced. The point here was that expanded tolerances may allow for lower-cost supplier processing. Often, product engineers had no real understanding of the cost differential associated with the different manufacturing processes that could be used to produce a particular part feature.

## Tying up Loose Ends

I hadn't let go the idea of wireform price reductions; that is, when costs go down prices go down. Wireform print review sessions lasted longer than the time needed for reviewing other part types due to the mixture between the art and science needed to produce them, as mentioned in the previous chapter.

I gave some thought to both wireform cost reduction and streamlining their review sessions and came up with the following idea.

*If product engineers understood the cost trade-offs between feature tolerance and cost up front, in the design they could properly match tolerance with part feature, lowering the part's cost prior to submitting them to print review. With this approach, the supplier could review tolerances beforehand, thus reducing the time of the print review sessions.*

I decided to see if the above were possible and to use wireforms as a test case. An important point here was that we would need supplier collaboration in putting a feature/tolerance/manufacturing feature/process cost manual with suppliers we had just put through a real-time online auction to keep their current business.

With this in mind, I wondered if any of our incumbent suppliers be interested collaborating with us in putting together such a manual.

We had one that agreed to help us with this. The only issue they had is that they didn't want to specify the actual manufacturing costs associated with the different processes relative to tolerance. We got around this by comparing costs using relative numbers. For instance, if the tightest tolerance—usually most expensive—could be expanded and, thus, could be manufactured by a less costly process—say 10 percent lower—we'd list that process as *90 percent* in the manual.

## The Result

A trial of the above changes in the wireform print review process was conducted; not only did it produce the hoped-for cost reductions, it also took about an hour off of the print review session times. An unanticipated impact of them was that it became easier to schedule wireform print review sessions due to the lower time commitment.

Though product design manuals wouldn't apply to all products, several others were put together.

## Summary

Print Reviews were a valuable part of the new part design release process. From a purchasing perspective, they were effective in reducing supplier manufacturing costs. But they were difficult to schedule due to the time commitment required from other functional areas.

We implemented a change that had not only continued to produce the needed financial results but also had substantially reduced the participant's time commitment. This led to easier scheduling of print review sessions.

## Change Rating

*Evolutionary*, since while the new process was tied to current practice, the impact was far beyond what was delivered by Incremental change.

## Lessons Learned

- Current processes, though effective, should be regularly evaluated for possible streamlining.
- As in manufacturing, reduction of *true* office lead-times also reduces waste.
- Impact can also be a differentiator between *Incremental, Evolutionary*, and *Revolutionary* changes.

# As a Materials Manager

# CHAPTER 16

# Supplier Selection Criteria

One of my first challenges upon becoming Materials Manager was to standardize a more comprehensive approach to sourcing decisions. I felt a primary principle should be that the person responsible for managing a future supplier should have the primary *say* regarding from whom to source purchased material. On the other hand, providing structure for their decisions is only prudent to ensure better choices.

The following describes the factors of consideration developed for supplier selection. They were first implemented in the mid-1990s, and I suspect there are many other criteria that should be added to this list, depending on market support needs. They certainly improved robustness of source selection in our department.

## Financial Strength

It must be confirmed up front that potential sources will be around for *the long run*. Consequently, they must have a positive balance sheet history.

## Company Ongoing Viability

If a potential supplier is a corporate entity, be familiar with their latest annual reports. If a supplier is privately held, try to learn things such as their annual revenue and their main customers. Resist giving a supplier business to either keep them afloat or help them launch a new business.

## Industry Knowledge

Suppliers with industry knowledge will have a better understanding of how to satisfy our customers and position us to compete in our markets more successfully.

## Characteristics of Our Market Demand

The markets of both OEMs where I worked were very seasonal. Suppliers need to either have capacity to support the peak demands or do so with prebuilt inventory, that is, waste. Knowledge of what will be their approach to this is important in understanding a supplier's operational capability.

## Knowledge of Our Competitors

This will give suppliers a better feel for what they must do to effectively support us in achieving our market-share targets. Correspondingly, we need to know those suppliers who supply both to us and our competitor(s). This knowledge is needed so we can work with them to ensure that they give us their best deal. At a minimum, suppliers should not charge us more than they do for anyone else they sold comparable products to.

## Ballpark Competitive Pricing

Pricing must always be a consideration in source selection and should be the primary factor when what is being purchased is a commodity. On the other hand, for noncommodity parts, the lowest quoted price should not be the sole—or even, in some cases, the primary—criteria for ensuring a supplier-based competitive advantage, When prices come at relatively similar levels, it may be better for overall performance to source with the more "local" supplier.

## Competitive Service Part Support

What is a potential supplier's pricing structure for service parts and what are their lead-times for them?

## Understanding of the Relationship between Specifications and Processing Costs

Producing parts *to spec* requires specific types of processing. Sometimes, part feature specifications can be adjusted to reduce the cost of this processing, for instance, by opening-up of tolerances on noncritical features.

Sharing this information during the design review process will allow us to align part safety, function, and reliability requirements with optimal processing cost.

## Cost Structure

Suppliers should be willing to share the cost of the materials they need to manufacture the parts and/or assemblies they sell, as well as the percentage of total part cost they make up. Knowing these two factors, however, gives us the ability to understand cost-reduction potential. For instance, the higher the material percentage, the lower the cost-reduction opportunities. It is less likely that suppliers will be willing to share cost factors such as employee wages, number of employees, overheads, and so on.

## A Focus on Continuous Improvement

This implies more than just having an internal continuous improvement function. It also includes a supplier's willingness to share their year-to-year cost-reduction history.

## A History of Effective Collaboration

This is an easy evaluation when a potential source is an incumbent supplier. For potential new sources, there are considerations that can be an indicator of whether a supplier has a focus on collaboration. For instance, suppliers should be willing to share generalized examples of collaborations they had with other customers.

## Process and Tooling Technology

There will always be instances where parts can be manufactured most effectively with older *tried-and-true* processes. But suppliers should also be aware of and evaluate newer manufacturing technology that may be just as or more effective and will result in processing cost reduction. A knowledge of their capital investment for the last 3 years as of the date of evaluation is a good indicator of this.

## Tooling Lead-times

It is important up front to know if the tooling a supplier uses to process our parts can be fabricated to align with new product development schedules.

## Prototype Lead-times

It is necessary to know whether supplier production of prototype part(s) will align with test-machine quantities.

## Will-Fit Service Parts Policy

A supplier must be willing to contractually agree that they will not manufacture and sell *will-fit* parts to compete with our own, branded service parts.

## Process Capability Approach to ensuring Quality

Here the issue is whether a potential source assures the delivery of parts-to-spec through inspection or through definition of process capability, that is, a statistical evaluation of whether a manufacturing process will deliver *on target and in-control* design specifications. The latter approach can be provided at less supplier cost and provides better assurance of quality while, at the same time, providing the customer the opportunity to reduce their Receiving Inspection costs and allow delivery of parts directly to their point of use.

## Supplier Capacity

Suppliers may have the ability to successfully develop and deliver prototype parts yet, when production starts up, are unable to support schedule quantities.

## Ability to Accept and Deliver Short-Fuse Schedule Changes

Does a potential supplier have the capability to cost-effectively deliver parts on a weekly or even daily basis? If so, do they do this through Lean practice or rely on prebuilt parts/assemblies?

## Onsite Support

There will always be supplier quality and order fulfillment issues that come up as part of ongoing operations. Quick response onsite supplier support is usually the most effective way to identify and resolve the root cause(s) of the problem. Not having this level of support increases the risk of production stoppages and has the potential to increase warranty or damaged-in-marketplace reputation issues.

## Summary

All sourcing decisions should be made by the person who will be responsible for the supplier's overall management. Providing a structure for guiding these decisions will lead to a higher-quality supplier consistently across all purchased material.

## Change Score

*Evolutionary*, since at this time OEMs were sourcing overseas based almost solely on piece-price. In my experience, they still do.

## Lessons Learned

- There are many factors that should be considered in the assessment and selection of suppliers, depending on business needs. Many will set the groundwork for purchasing to increase its positive impact above and beyond material cost to their company's bottom line.
- In selecting sources, buyers should be able to understand and define any potential supplier process shortfalls that could negatively affect performance.
- Formalizing and documenting of these potential capability shortfalls is an important step in supplier selection.

# CHAPTER 17

# Supplier Order Fulfillment

## An Obsolete Model

OEM order fulfillment policies are set to define supplier performance expectations for market-demand scenarios that are likely to occur during the normal course of business.

As previously described, reducing waste by prioritizing reduction of strategic supplier's *true* lead-times became our Unit's primary supplier development strategy. Unfortunately, our factory's order fulfillment policy gave suppliers a 90-day firm commitment. This meant that if suppliers built ahead of our schedule(s), we would buy the quantity of parts in a 90-day rolling forecast—"even if we had no use for them"—for instance, in cases where market-demand forecasts were lower than consumer demand.

This *Firm Zone* had been originally established based on the premise that the longer the firm commitment—that is, giving suppliers a more stable schedule—the better chance they could minimize manufacturing costs. In point of fact, though, it also encouraged them to set their response time at 90 days—which meant they were building their own finished goods inventory to support *true* lead-times.

In fact, in working with our suppliers to assess their *true* lead-times we found that many, indeed, had *true* lead-times approaching or even exceeding 90 days. Our own schedules were based on forecasts, and, in our industry, forecasts historically contained significant errors. This essentially meant a lot of supplier development work would be required to reduce supplier *true* lead-times such that they could better support market dynamics, that is, change/reduce our 90-day Firm Commitment Policy.

## Laying the Groundwork for the Upgrade

To revise these guidelines, purchasing would need to define, justify, engage, and gain buy-in from both suppliers and other impacted functional areas within our own organization. A strong business case met this need internally, and showing suppliers we were only asking them to do what we were already doing—*do as I do*—went a long way toward convincing them a change was needed. It was also pretty apparent to suppliers that should they not go along with our new commitment policy, they risked losing business.

There was a history of suppliers not being able to support our short-fuse schedule changes. Many times—despite firefighting efforts—they couldn't or weren't willing to add the cost needed to do so to their manufacturing process since this would lower their own profit margins. As a consequence, while our production schedule would be revised to consider actual supplier response capability, it would only partially align with market demand. In addition, because of our 90-day Firm Commitment Policy, supplier performance would not take a hit in either of these two above situations.

On the internal marketing side, I found that prebuilt finished goods inventory quantities were set without understanding supply-base capabilities. Marketing performance metrics included Customer Fill Rate (the percentage of time a product was available when a customer was willing to buy it). Because of this, they tended to overestimate the amount of prebuilt finished goods inventory needed to maintain it. This, of course, ignored the most important factor in calculating the needed quantity. And perhaps more importantly, it became a barrier to the goal of reducing a reliance on prebuilt, finished goods inventory.

To establish a business case for determining the needed supplier flexibility, I worked with our factory scheduler to see how well our support—or failure to support—market demand varied from past forecasts. We looked at the last 10 years of this, and what we found out wasn't good. For instance, there were years when demand came in over 25 percent higher than was forecast in either total or for SKU-specific product that in no case had we been able to increase production by more than 8 percent in our efforts to satisfy it. And this was primarily due to lack of supplier agility.

I had a discussion with a Marketing Vice-President laying out this data. He told me that it was our job to fix the supply-base such that they were prepared to instantaneously respond to unlimited changes in our schedule.

It became evident as our discussion proceeded that this expectation was not possible. To his credit, the Marketing VP then asked,

"What type of supplier reaction would be necessary to maintain Customer Fill Rates if it was not based on prebuilt, finished goods inventory?"

I laid out further data that our scheduler and I had put together quantifying lost sales data. Specifically, we found that if suppliers—with 2 weeks' notice—could deliver up to 20 percent more than was in the rolling 3-month schedule, we could have captured 95 percent of the lost sales over that same 10-year period. Based on the data, Marketing agreed that if we could make this happen, they would be willing to significantly reduce their stocks of prebuilt, finished goods inventory since, theoretically anyway, doing so would not reduce their Customer Fill Rates.

## New Parameter Definition and Implementation

We justified internally that to increase supply-base agility would require 3 years. To implement this change, we rolled out what the new firm commitment would be.

- A 2-week *Firm Zone*, during which we committed to not changing our production schedules.
- A 90-day *Trade-Off Zone*, during which suppliers would be expected to deliver 20 percent above what was in the previously issued quarterly forecast.
- A *Forecast Zone*, after which suppliers need to be able to support changes in orders up to the consuming OEM's factory capacity.

Our following *Order Change Policy* ended up as follows.

| Zone | Duration | Flexibility |
|------|----------|-------------|
| Firm | Thru 14 days | 0% |
| Trade-Off | 15 thru 90 days | 20% |
| Forecast | 90+ days | Our factory's maximum capacity |

In recognition of the magnitude of what this change represented, it would to be phased in over 3 years, as follows:

| Current state | 90-days-firm zone |
| --- | --- |
| Year 1 | 60-days-firm zone |
| Year 2 | 30-days-firm zone |
| Year 3 | 14-days-firm zone |

Also, in recognition of the magnitude of this change, supplier development support was offered to facilitate it. In the end, over 80 strategic suppliers requested and received support in reducing their *true* lead-times. One of the first steps was to help suppliers define them. This was necessary because most suppliers had no idea of what their *true* lead-times were.

At the end of the 3-year implementation schedule, the average *true* lead-times of these 80 suppliers were reduced by 80 percent. And as a result of this, many of the impacted suppliers reduced their internal waste to the point where they were able to offer significant price reductions.

The next discussion was with production control. I found that our factory didn't have a specifically defined maximum capacity either in total or SKU production, which is a critical element in managing supplier order fulfillment flexibility. We calculated and quantified this for our suppliers. This was a critical element in their own order fulfillment planning.

The upshot may be that your suppliers—at least out of the chute—may not have the capability of supporting the Firm, Flex, and Forecast Zone requirements you require to meet your Customer Fill Rate goals. By changing the order fulfillment policy based on actual business needs, they now had rational business-based targets to shoot for.

To accommodate the gap between supplier agility and the standards outlined in our new policy, suppliers may need some built-ahead finished goods contingency inventory. Our position was this was due to their lack of order fulfillment agility. Consequently, we would make no commitment to buy it; nor would we entertain a price-increase request because of their costs of maintaining it.

## Summary

A major change in our customer order fulfillment strategy would be a requirement to successfully market our products through the Big Box merchandizing channel. A large part of this change would involve significant supplier *true* lead-time reduction. Associated with this, we would need to significantly reduce our 90-day Firm Commitment Policy.

Based on historical data, we were able to show that a 2-week Firm Commitment Policy—after which a supplier could be asked for a 20 percent upward flex above what was in the originally issued 3-month rolling schedule—would reduce *lost sales* by about 95 percent.

To somewhat reduce the challenge of this significant change, we phased the change in over 3 years as well as offered supplier development support, as requested.

## Change Rating

*Revolutionary*, since we were in effect adding a completely new supplier capability to our supplier performance assessments and, in reducing the *true* lead-times of our supply-base, created what turned out to be a significantly successful business strategy.

## Lessons Learned

- Creating a new business model can greatly increase competitiveness. In this case, it meant completely changing the way in which we managed our suppliers.
- Significant effort must be made to create a business model justifying both the change and the implementation schedule. Internally, people weren't happy with having to wait 3 years for the change to occur, but I was able to show based on data that it would require that amount of time to facilitate increased supply-base order fulfillment agility.

- To be successful in facilitating such a transition, changes will need to be coordinated across different operational functions, breaking down, in effect, the walls of the purchasing silo.
- The change would not have been either possible or successful without a functioning supplier development resource.

# CHAPTER 18

# The New VP and His Directors

We in the purchasing community were encouraged—especially Unit Material Managers—when we found out that a well-known and respected purchasing executive was being brought in from another company to be Corporate Vice-President of Purchasing. He would be reporting to the CEO. This, we felt, would give purchasing the visibility needed to gain acceptance as a strategic—rather than tactical—corporate function. Based on his reputation as a promoter of collaborative practices, we assumed that the new VP's strategies would align with how we currently were operating. Later, we would find that this expectation was wrong.

Unfortunately, I later had to give him the nick-name *Imposter*.

## The Four Horsemen of the Apocalypse

Imposter brought in four new Directors, with one stationed at the corporate office and the others positioned to oversee the purchasing function in three of the company's four divisions, that is, not the one where I worked. For the same reasons outlined above, Unit Material Managers were enthused since we felt these individuals could introduce *new perspectives* based on how they operated at their previous employers.

We, however, became less enthused when it became apparent that the strategies and practices they brought in were more positional than collaborative. They also seemed to assume that their role was to enforce strategies and practices coming out of corporate, leaving little room for Unit contributions to their development.

# The Fourth Horseman—Supplier Development *Death*

For example, one such practice was to propose operating the company's supplier development function along the lines of General Motors' (GM) PICOS (Program for Improvement and Cost Optimization of Suppliers). PICOS was instituted at GM by their head of purchasing, Jose Ignacio Lopez de Arriortua, who was known for his assertive style of dealing with suppliers.

PICOS was based on a team of GM employees auditing a supplier's operations to identify and financially quantify areas of waste. After that, they would both leave the supplier on their own in removing that waste and, at the same time, apply all of the projected waste elimination to instantaneous material cost reduction leaving no benefit to the supplier. Of course, much of the projected waste was not real, so the supplier ended up with reduced margins for undergoing the entire process.

Suppliers were not given a choice as to whether or not to participate in the program.

I was familiar with PICOS and had, in fact, talked to several GM suppliers upon whom the process had been imposed. They felt that PICOS was predatory rather than collaborative. They said they felt uncomfortable that GM's auditors unilaterally assumed the authority to financially quantify the cost reductions associated with the identified waste. They also felt calling PICOS *supplier development* was an inappropriate usage of the term.

At the time, our Division's supplier development function was made up of only three employees. I was extremely proud of their work, which demonstrated that our collaborative and project facilitation process delivered internal savings for us above and beyond what could have been associated with win-lose negotiations. Suppliers shared in any savings associated with the removed waste, that is, a win-win result. And different from PICOS—a program GM suppliers only reluctantly agreed to participate in—our Divisional suppliers lined up for supplier development support once the results of our initial facilitations had been shared at our next annual supplier conference.

GM discarded PICOS as a primary strategy for material cost reduction when its win-lose, leverage-focused Chief Purchasing Officer died.

I find it interesting to note that several years later, GM's new focus on collaboration led to their top-most rating in multiple annual supplier surveys of OEM customer progressive practices.

The reason I've laid out PICOS in so much detail is because one of the Directors was from GM and considered himself a supplier development guru. While he was given responsibility for purchasing strategies and practices at one of our company's Divisions, he had also hoped to be the named leader of supplier development efforts across the entire company. Of course, he planned to model our company's supplier development process after PICOS.

A red flag went immediately up in my mind in my first interaction with him. We discussed both PICOS results and the price reduction result our three-person supplier development group had delivered the previous year, which was about $9 million in price reductions; that is, the actual cost reduction was greater than this, but, as previously stated, an important part of our supplier development strategy was to share any savings with the supplier. I pointed out to him that this *carrot-type* approach greatly overcame any reservations suppliers had about our offering supplier development support and, as a result, demand for suppliers requesting such support enabled me to justify increasing the size of the supplier development group.

His response was along the lines of:

"Well, that is good. In my last year with GM, I was involved in nearly $1,000,000,000 in price reductions." Later, in learning how PICOS worked, I understood how such results could be obtained.

## A Difference in Strategies

An example of the PICOS approach to supplier development was given visibility during the question-and-answer period of a corporate-wide supplier development conference. A Buyer asked whether they should feel free to use supplier information that supplier development people had learned about to gain leverage in their piece-price negotiations. The new Director responded "yes," as per the PICOS handbook.

I then stood up and answered the question by saying that in our Division we signed an MOU before starting a supplier engagement project. It laid out—among other things—that the supplier would own all project-related information and that none will be shared with people outside of the project team—including our own internal personnel—without the supplier's consent.

Edward Deming once said:

*The result of long-term relationships is better quality, and lower and lower costs.*

I decided to side myself with Deming on this issue rather than GM's Chief Procurement Officer.

On the other hand, some other Materials Managers did drink the Lopez *Kool-Aid*, at least to some extent. For instance, in talking with a colleague from another Division, I explained my position that the primary strategy of supplier management should be developing suppliers. He replied this perspective was *nonsense* and stuck to positional negotiating and resourcing overseas to obtain the price reductions that Corporate was asking for.

## A Strategy in Name Only

Another issue was that none of the new Directors understood the demand parameters of the markets the different Divisions of our company served and, perhaps even worse, seemed to think that this didn't matter in the development of purchasing strategies and practices.

We came to understand that, in his presentation to our Board of Directors, Imposter had significantly overpromised the positive impacts purchasing could have on company financials. His primary strategy, he said, would be to adopt a more coordinated approach with product development, operations, and marketing functions.

Contrary to this I never saw him, or his new Directors, contact any of my Division's functional teams:

- Product engineering function, to better understand the operational aspects or the performance our customers expected from our products.

- Our operations function, to better understand the history of the schedule changes that our Unit needed to make to align production with market demand in quantity or SKU mix.
- Marketing function, to better understand the varying demand characteristics and seasonality of our marketplace.

Bottom line, they would have discovered that our products and markets were significantly different from those of corporation's other three Divisions and, because of this, the need for developing sourcing and purchasing strategies in support of those differences.

## Summary

The new purchasing regime attempted to implement a non-collaborative company-wide cookie-cutter approach to purchasing. This was not appropriate due to our Division's purchasing culture, unique product lines, and its variable market-demand characteristics. Because of this, we resisted their one-size-fits-all strategy and process premise.

## Change Rating

*Evolutionary*, though in this case the rating was based on resistance to *inappropriate* change.

## Lessons Learned

- Anticipated positive contributions to strategy and practice are not always delivered by *new blood*. Caution should be taken when those they propose seem to offer unrealistic results.
- Changes should not be adopted for change's sake. Corporate-wide cookie-cutter strategies and processes have the potential to be inappropriate for a company whose businesses cover diverse product lines and compete in varying markets.
- When publicly challenging a company executive, do not criticize. Rather, lay out your position in a neutral way and let the audience make their own personnel decision on which position to support.

# CHAPTER 19

# Corporate Consolidations

I've spent most of my industrial career working on jobs related to factory operations and have really enjoyed it. A basic tenet of this book is that change management is a key element for improving overall company competitiveness. And that this could best be accomplished at operational factories.

At the Units where I 've worked, however, it seemed like there were always a few colleagues who would do anything and everything to position themselves for *a Job at Corporate*. This meant not taking risks that could result in negative visibility. So very few of them acted as *change agents*.

In my opinion, this was because corporate employees acted as though they had more control over strategy and processes yet could avoid facing real-life issues encountered in a factory environment. That was certainly my experience with the new corporate purchasing regime.

I agree that there can be benefits to having a corporate purchasing function. A rationale often used in support of this is the need for a company to project a single face to suppliers. When a corporation is comprised of multiple Divisions buying from one supplier, there are business reasons for ensuring that some supplier interactions should be standardized. Their development is usually facilitated by corporate, one goal of which is to define and combine the middle-ground *best-fit* elements with existing Unit's purchasing practices.

## Corporate Guidance

The rub, however, comes when corporate—on its own—mandates new purchasing strategies and processes without participation and input from the Units.

Consolidating control of purchasing decisions at corporate can be counterproductive, *especially* when that group promotes itself as the company's exclusive controlling authority, de-emphasizing the role of Unit purchasing groups. This tends to set the tone that Unit procurement is tactical while that of the corporate group is strategic.

Our Division manufactured completely different product types and competed in a market considerably different to those of our other three Divisions. This implied that many of our purchases should be sourced from suppliers with capabilities different than those needed by the other three Divisions. Because of this, for the most part, there was a wide disparity between supply-bases.

Care must be taken in setting up a corporate procurement function to not consolidate control to the point that it gets in the way of Units making good industry-specific business decisions, including how to select sources that can best service their customer demand. Corporate functions that are not set up this way can cause more harm than good.

Below I'll explain a couple of failed corporate sourcing strategy mistakes.

## Examples of Corporate Sourcing Done Wrong

There is a whole array of sourcing nightmare stories I could relate. The bottom line is I've seen many, many instances where corporate purchasing put together what they considered to be a good sourcing strategy that, if implemented, would end up having negative impacts at the Unit or Divisional level.

## Example 1

The first example of this can be found in tire sourcing. One day, as the Unit Materials Manager, I got a phone call from Corporate telling me that they were taking over the sourcing of all company tire purchases. Their justification for this was that our Division's tire usage dwarfed that of the other Divisions. For instance, during high-demand sales seasons, we needed about 2 million tires a year to keep our production lines running. Demand in the other Divisions could be satisfied by—at most—by annual volumes in the tens of thousands.

The thought was to combine the tire volumes of all of the company's Divisions into a single *buy* to get leverage in pricing negotiations.

There were two main problems with this strategy. First, the materials and manufacturing processes used to produce our Division's tires were completely different than those used for manufacturing tires in the other Divisions.

Second, there was no single manufacturer in the world that produced tires that could be used by both our products and the products produced in the other three Divisions. One reason for this was because the other Division's products—for the most part—were very large, weighing up to several tons and used in vastly different tough off-road operating environments.

Our products, on the other hand, were very small and much lower in weight. The target customer was the homeowner/consumer, not a challenging operating environment.

It didn't surprise me that this was new information to the new Corporate Sourcing Manager. After all, he did not have background in the specifications of our Division's tires, compared to those used in the other Divisions; nor did he have knowledge of tire manufacturing.

## Example 2

The second example involved a simple stamped and welded bracket. Our company had a process that compared current part designs for similarity. If two parts were found to be similar, there would be an attempt to adjust the design of one, the other, or both such that the annual requirements for the revised parts would be greater than for either part on its own. The thought behind this approach was that doing so could increase leverage in supplier price negotiations as well as reduce the number of service parts and service part inventory the company would need to retain and maintain.

Again, as a Unit Materials Manager, I got a call one day from the corporate person assigned to design consolidation. He explained that they had found a similar part used by both our Unit and another Division. They had then worked directly with both Divisional Product Engineering departments (unbeknownst to me) to tweak the designs of both parts into a single, common one that would be functionally effective in both products.

In addition, they had sent out a Request for Quote based on our combined annual requirements to both current suppliers, that is, our domestic and the other Division's overseas source. It turned out that sourcing the combined quantity with the overseas supplier would result in a price reduction of about 12 percent, significantly better than the price quoted by our domestic supplier.

I replied that this sounded good but told him I had a few questions. First, what were the Quality and On-time Delivery performance metrics of the overseas supplier? Since this supplier already manufactured parts for our company, he was able to give me an answer that they had excellent performance in both metrics.

The second was, would this supplier be able to support short-fuse variations in demand differing—both in SKU and/or total volume—from what had been forecast? He seemed a bit confused by the question. He said that the supplier's delivery performance indicated they could. I replied that this really didn't answer my question.

I explained market demand for our products was quite variable and a result of this was that our forecasts typically contained significant amounts of errors. I went on to tell him that our sales season was quite seasonal, with two-thirds of our sales occurring in three consecutive months of the year. This meant that the forecast error could only be mediated by quickly changing schedules. This, in turn, meant that our Division had to source to suppliers with order fulfillment agility since sourcing parts from those who lack such ability would result in lost sales. And that the response capability we needed was delivery of the new order volumes to our Unit within 2 weeks of the schedule change notification.

He responded to this by saying the schedule change requirement in the other Divisions was 90 days. He went on to say that he thought our requirement was severe and probably not needed. I explained that demand in other Division's markets was fairly level over a year. And that this meant their forecasts were at least a magnitude more accurate than our forecasts, implying that they didn't need suppliers that could support short-fuse changes. Added to that, their customer base was willing to wait weeks or months for a product that was not currently available. On the other hand, our customers would typically wait only days—or at most a week—for a product currently not in stock at our retailers.

He told me he thought this shouldn't be a problem since, although the source's lead-time was 90 days, we could compensate for this by ordering the *best-case* demand requirements ahead of our 3 months sales season and use any of the inventoried parts that were left over in subsequent sales periods. In our case, it would be at best 9 months later.

I replied that there were reasons we would not do this. First, if there were quality problems with the preordered raw material inventory, the overseas supplier could not replenish them in time to meet our sales window. Second, due to associated costs, we were not willing to hold 9 months of raw material inventory waiting for the next sales season. Third, since in our industry there were almost annual design changes to or complete redesign of products, there was a fair chance that the inventoried parts might not be needed following the current sales season. For all of these reasons, we had to turn down Corporate's proposal.

## Corporate and Unit Roles in a Company-wide Strategy

What's to be done? Should we just forget about corporate purchasing and make every purchasing strategy/sourcing decision locally? Absolutely not!

There definitely is a role for a corporate purchasing function at most companies. But there should also be limits set in the control they have in the sourcing decisions. The most important of these is to understand the market-demand fluctuations of all product categories. This knowledge would be difficult to obtain and maintain by corporate purchasing departments, especially given employee turnover. On the other hand, at our factory, two people were assigned to each product category so there would essentially be no loss in continuity should one of them move on.

Bottom line, I saw very little opportunity to consolidate factory purchases except in commodities.

## Summary

Our Division's products had drastically different design and demand criteria from the products manufactured and sold by other Divisions within our company. The two cases described above sought to combine our annual requirements with those of other Divisions to increase negotiating leverage. However, their proposals were for us to resource to suppliers without the capabilities to meet our schedule change needs. We put together a business case justifying our nonparticipation in these two new corporate sourcing proposals.

## Change Rating

*Evolutionary.* Sourcing is sourcing, but it was shown that suppliers need to compete for business base on Unit and Divisional product needs.

## Lessons Learned

- Corporate centralization of sourcing does make sense for commodities. But for the most part, it does not, for designed parts.
- Most purchasing consolidations I've seen work to reduce overall manpower by adding people at corporate and dramatically reducing Unit manpower. There was no doubt in my mind that a power grab—rather than logic—is at the root of the effort to consolidate sourcing at corporate. In the end, moves such as these would mean that corporate has strategic control while Units became solely tactical.
- Consolidation can move the development and implementation of purchasing strategies and processes farther away from the customer, which limits purchasing ability to successfully support the marketplace.

# CHAPTER 20

# Common Sense and Teamwork

In a book attributed (authored by a ghost author) to Imposter and Darth, our company was called out as having a *World-Class* supplier development function. What it was really saying is that *our* Division's supplier development function was *World-Class*. This was because the three other Division's in our company—while they had added supplier development resources—struggled with developing their overall strategy. Consequently, they hadn't developed the tools needed to produce the magnitude positive financial results being delivered by our group.

This was noticed and acknowledged across the corporation. To address this gap, the newly hired Directors from the other three Divisions suggested that we should standardize supplier development strategies and processes/tools across the company. This would be accomplished through a series of supplier development tool and process-focused classes, and it seemed to me to be a good idea.

## A Supplier Development Academy?

It was interesting that while nine classes were eventually decided on, there was still no agreement on an overall supplier development strategy. In my experience, it should usually be the other way around.

It turned out that two-thirds of the training classes were instruction on tools that my supplier development group had developed and regularly used. Consequently, those classes would be taught by people from our group. They were to be held during the first two weeks of a three-week training session. Those taught by supplier development engineers from other Divisions would be held during the third.

Our Division's supplier development function was staffed by nine individuals, primarily masters-prepared industrial engineers. It was proposed that all company supplier development engineers attend each training class.

I was concerned about the unbudgeted out-or-pocket costs my group would incur. For instance, I would have had to pay for food, travel, and lodging since the training was to take place off-site from our factory. And this was despite all of our Division's supplier development engineers being familiar with and having implemented the tools to be reviewed during the first 2 weeks of instruction. This didn't seem to be right.

## The Issue of Cost

Including me in our group's increased the number of employees in it to 10. Three weeks of classes (15 days)—times 10 rooms a night equals 150 hotel nights. Assuming an average of $100 per night results in an overall cost of $15,000. I estimated food and travel to average $100 per day, which would double that cost to $30,000.

I was not actively involved in actual supplier development facilitation, so the 15-class days would only take away 135 days of resources to support ongoing supplier development projects, delaying the potential benefits from those facilitations. Based on past results, the daily financial benefit from a project typically was around $2,500 per day of engagement. Having my supplier development engineers attend each class the first 2 weeks of training would result in delay of $22,500 potential price reductions. While not an out-of-pocket cost, it was still a factor in my consideration.

To mediate the above, I suggested to the three Directors that if an individual supply development engineer could point to having successfully implemented project work using a particular tool, that person would not have to attend training in that tool.

This idea was struck down since they felt that there needed to be a show of *unity* among supplier development resources across the corporation.

This response angered me, so I decided to do what was right for my Division, as well as the company. Consequently, our Division's nine supplier development employees and I would only attend the 5 days of training put on by the other Divisions. This would result in reducing hotel and living expenses about $20,000. Factoring back in the 5 days—each—of training that would be conducted by two of our engineers would add back in $2,000, reducing the overall savings to $18,000.

## Poking the Corporate IM&S in the Eye with a Stick

But I was not done. Although it was the responsibility of the Corporate Indirect Materials and Services group (IM&S) to negotiate daily rates with hotel chains, I felt that by guaranteeing 60 *room days* of occupancy—which included our engineers who would deliver the initial 2 weeks of training—we might be able to negotiate rates below those that the Corporate group had delivered.

To try out this theory, we had a contest among the group as to who could negotiate the best room rate based on that commitment.

We were able to negotiate a daily room rate 30 percent lower than the corporate rate with a hotel that was part of a chain that corporate had already negotiated with. Why? It was the tourist/travel offseason, and there were rooms available that would normally remain empty during the period we'd be staying there; that is, the primary metric—besides revenue—a hotel manager is rated on is daily *percent occupancy*. This was win-win for both my budget and the hotel manager.

With the 30 percent discount we were able to take $5,400 out of the lodging cost! Our overall out-of-pocket expenses were reduced to $12,600 from the original $30,000 in room, board, and transportation out-of-pocket expenses.

Unfortunately, that wasn't the end of the story.

Corporate IM&S found out about our hotel rate reduction and because of it they took us to the *woodshed*. They explained that they had responsibility for negotiating hotel rates for the corporation and that we were out-of-bounds in doing what we had done. I asked if they had considered seasonality in their negotiations and received no direct answer, which led me to believe that they hadn't. I was given a strict dictate that going forward we would adhere to Corporate-negotiated lodging rates.

I decided not to fight this battle but wondered if the IM&S group would learn from this experience or not. I never heard if they did.

# Summary

My supplier development group was looking at a significant out-of-pocket expense relative to an upcoming series of training classes. It was also looking at a delay in ongoing projects, which had the potential to delay the delivery of positive financial impacts to our corporation. We were able to reduce the out-of-budget costs significantly as well as continue to support most of our ongoing supplier development project work. This was based on a change in our group's classroom attendance that the Directors of the other three Divisions weren't happy with and *undercutting* (their word) Corporate IM&S responsibility.

# Change Rating

None, our Division saved insignificant, nonrecurring savings.

# Lessons Learned

- Being a team player is important, but not when unneeded expense can be avoided.
- Through the training we provided, supplier development engineers from the company's other three Division's gained an understanding that there were existing tools that could be used to simplify and expand the impact of their work.
- I was to find out later that the primary supplier development performance metric at the other three Divisions remained short-term material cost reduction, and, because of this, several of those tools were never fully utilized. The lesson here was that performance metrics need to change to facilitate changes in employee activity.

Not aligning with current practices can be seen as threatening by individuals responsible for current practice. I'm pretty sure that one of the other three Divisional Directors had mentioned what we did with IM&S. When you make a change in your area of responsibility, but will not likely impact a wider practice, it is probably the best to keep it under-the-carpet to avoid an experience like we had with corporate IM&S.

# CHAPTER 21

# Holding Companies as Suppliers

One of the largest challenges in launching a supplier development function is finding those initial suppliers who will accept an offer of assistance. This is because over time, the win-lost negotiation strategy used by many OEMs has reduced the trust factor between them and their suppliers. An example of this is shown by how one supplier put it to me:

> *When one of my OEM customers tells me they want to collaborate, I put my hand over my wallet because, based on experience, I know that they are usually after my money.*

## Holding Companies

One day I learned that one of our small, family-owned suppliers—who had agreed to a supplier development engagement-had been purchased by a Holding Company. I was a bit concerned because I had stories about how Holding Companies operated, none of them good.

A day or two later I was in this Holding Company's home office laying out the parameters, framework, and terms of our supplier development assistance. Their CFO had heard of our supplier development program, said they were moving their operation and asked for our help in designing and developing a new *greenfield* factory layout.

I explained to the Holding Company's CFO that based on our design and implementation support we expected to receive a half-share of the cost reduction results in the form of piece-price reductions, which he agreed to.

# A Surprise and Denial

He contacted the incumbent factory manager who was now going to be the manager of the new facility, and who I had enjoyed a long relationship with. He told me that the Holding Company's corporate executives said that for the supplier development support to proceed, the savings ratio would need to be changed, that is, with them getting the larger part.

I answered "no."

I said that if his bosses wanted to play *hardball*, I would immediately institute the *90-Day Notice of Severance Clause* that was in our boilerplate, which was considered part of a contract by the Uniform Commercial Code and would allow us to resource our business away from them.

I also reminded him that during the 90-day transition period they would be obligated to maintain regular supply to us, also as per the boiler plate. Since we represented almost 20 percent of annual revenue of their factory, I knew that my action would create shockwaves back at the Holding Company's home office.

The home office did get back to me and said they'd honor the original cost-reduction-sharing agreement. Consequently, our supplier development group engaged with them and oversaw implementation of the manufacturing layout of their new factory.

This whole episode had left a bad taste in my mouth, so I met one last time with Holding Company's executives. I told him that we had spent years developing a trusting, collaborative working relationship with the supplier's previous ownership and that much of that trust had been destroyed over the last half-year because of their organization's unethical behavior.

After the supplier development engagement was complete, I told the Holding Company executives that going forward, my company was open to working with them to reestablish a trusting, collaborative working relationship, but that they had to re-earn this status. And, until they had, we would be working with them on a commercial win-lose basis. Based on what had occurred with their attempting to renege on our cost-sharing agreement, they knew I had all the leverage.

They didn't like this, but I told them they'd have to live with it.

## A Holding Company's Long-Term Play

I came away from this whole experience with an understanding that Holding Companies purchased small- and medium-sized manufacturers with one goal in mind. Specifically, to cosmetically clean up their balance sheet such that they can then sell the company for a handsome profit. And, in doing so, they were willing to do anything—ethical or not—to make this happen, including attempting to take advantage of their acquisition's current customer base.

## Summary

One of our family-owned strategic suppliers was sold to a Holding Company. This was my first—but not last—experience working with that type of organization. We had agreed to a supplier development engagement with the previous ownership, and the Holding Company said they wanted to proceed with it. They then told me that they were going to renege on our collaborative cost-sharing agreement. We didn't accept their bullying, and they backed off of their position.

## Change Rating

*Evolutionary*, since it demonstrated to me that it was in the DNA of Holding Companies to operate in a commercial win-lose manner, including with incumbent customers. Perhaps this approach may work with small- and medium-sized customers, but my employer was a large corporation, was their factory's largest customer, had an alternate Plan B sourcing strategy, and probably had more lawyers than they did! This was likely a rude awakening to them and probably led to a change in their company acquisition criteria—don't purchase a manufacturer whose primary customer is a larger OEM.

A result of this experience was that my group, in future work with Holding Companies, used our leverage to negotiate lower pricing. Unfortunately, going forward, we had several more experiences with these types of organizations.

## Lessons Learned

- Holding Companies are more interested in increasing short-term profits of their purchases—regardless of how their actions negatively impacted them over the long run—so as to present the façade that they owned a highly desirable manufacturing firm.
- Holding Companies are not interested in developing a collaborative relationship with their customers. Instead, they operate in a win-lose manner which they expect to always be on the winning side.
- In their interactions with customers, Holding Companies assume that they hold a greater amount of the overall leverage and, based on this, use it aggressively. This is not always the case—even with small- and medium-sized customers—and, when it isn't, the customer should turn the tables on their bullying supplier.
- Holding Company executives take Milton Friedman's philosophy to the extreme, probably since *they* represent a large portion of their company's ownership. This enhances their drive to do anything—ethical or unethical—to increase the purchase's commercial value.

# CHAPTER 22

# Application Makes All the Difference

Roto-Molding involves a heated mold that is filled with a shot of semi-melted material. It is then slowly rotated—usually around two perpendicular axes—causing the softened material to disperse and stick to the inside walls of the mold, forming a hollow part. The material used can be very robust, which is needed for stressful applications. The mold, then, continues to rotate during the cooling phase to avoid sagging or deformation. The overall process to produce a single fuel tank is a relatively slow process, sometimes taking over an hour per part.

Roto-Molding tooling and processing equipment are relatively inexpensive, and, due to its slow processing, multiple sets are usually required to support actual market demand. But this isn't much of a negative factor when customer production needs are small.

The above fit in nicely with the applications in the other three Divisions. Product demand was low—usually in the low five single-digit thousands—and the robust material and wall thickness needed for each of the finished product applications could be specified. Our Division was a latecomer to the company. Primarily, due the existing Roto-Molding usage and the long-term collaborative supplier relationship that had been established, fuel tanks for our products were also designed for Roto-Molding processing.

Our products were different from those produced in the other Divisions. Ours primarily targeted homeowners' usage while their products were designed for commercial users. Our production numbers were magnitudes higher, and our current supplier did not have the capacity to support our narrow, peak-demand period. For this reason, we built ahead significant amounts of inventory because if demand that came in was above forecast we'd lose sales.

# The Decision

To make a long story short, the decision was made that Injection-Molded Fuel Tanks were a better fit for our products and sufficiently robust to operate in our product's relatively low-stress duty cycles. It was true that while Injection-Molding tooling and processing equipment is significantly more expensive, we would need only a single set due to Injection Molding's having a short manufacturing cycle time. Making this switch would not only deliver the flexibility needed to support market demand more efficiently and effectively but also result in a significant fuel tank price reduction as well as a significantly lower need for fuel tank inventory.

We had made the Roto-Molding supplier aware of the pending change well before it would be made, and, while he didn't like the decision, it was difficult for him to criticize the business decision.

Prior to implementing the change, I reviewed the underlying business case and was given the "ok" to go ahead and make the change. So far so good!

This created somewhat of a crisis within our company since the supplier had previously been the sole source of fuel tanks. It also was a huge economic blow to the supplier since our volumes represented a significant part of their overall production.

I was asked if my actions were ethically justified. My answer was "perhaps." But I would add to that my feeling that the real tragedy was with the person who had sourced the fuel tanks with a higher-cost supplier that lacked the capabilities needed to support our markets.

# Summary

I and my team had proposed and successfully implemented a sourcing change that resulted in significant savings and higher Customer Fill Rates for my Division. This caused as major rift within the company as this action resulted in a significant loss of income from a long-term, collaborative company that had previously supplied fuel tanks to our entire enterprise.

## Change Rating

*Evolutionary.* We were willing to step forward and change an earlier mistaken sourcing strategy. We deviated from company standard practice but, at the same time, saved our Division a significant amount of money.

## Lessons Learned

- I personally knew the owner the Roto-Molding supplier and felt terrible about having to make a move that would so severely damage his business. But I also recognized not doing so would be a barrier to increasing our Division's marketplace competitiveness.
- My normal approach when resourcing from a long-term collaborative supplier is to give them a period of time to adjust their business such that they are able to adjust to the new market realities. Here, though, the financial benefits were too great and the probability of their successfully making such an adjustment was too low to maintain status quo.

# CHAPTER 23

# Supplier Training Consortium

One important part of supplier development is to *teach suppliers how-to-fish*. Effective facilitation of supplier development cost-reduction projects rely on supplier personnel understanding manufacturing basics as well as the tools they'll need to identify and reduce waste. This training, and the experience they gain during project implementation also lays a good foundation for future internal supplier cost-reduction activities after the completion of the supplier development engagement.

There are two basic barriers to supporting supplier manufacturing cost reduction, the first being a lack of supplier development resources. With dozens or hundreds of strategic suppliers targeted for engagement, it is unreasonable to think that an OEM customer can have enough supplier development engineers to assist all of them in short order.

The second is that a supply-base is typically made up of well over 50 percent of small- and medium-sized manufacturers. Employees of such firms do not typically have an understanding of the ABCs of Lean, Quality Control, Order Fulfillment, and so on. Training them in these areas would represent a huge commitment by both suppliers (due to employee time away from job and costs associated with training, that is, fees, travel, lodging, and meals) and OEMs, whose supplier development resources would be tasked with teaching it.

Outside training support takes two primary forms. The first is by an outside consultant. In this circumstance, fees are based on both consultant's time spent—up to thousands of dollars a day—as well as the number of participants involved in the training, typically in the range of $50 to $200 per person, as of the publishing of this book. These costs are often out of the reach of small- and medium-sized manufacturers.

The second is to train at publicly funded educational institutions, such as technical colleges and universities. When these sources of training are not local to a supplier—although the training cost is usually lower than with consultants—the supplier is still stuck with financing travel, lodging, and meals. This, again, puts the cost of training outside the budget of many small- and medium-sized manufacturers.

## A Bit of Training Reality

I have an interesting personal experience involving this issue. A supplier firm with about 100 employees reached out to us for supplier development assistance. When I broached the topic of whether his employees had training in the fundamentals of manufacturing cost reduction, he answered "no." He confirmed the reason for this was budgetary. He then asked how much would be needed to get the necessary training. My response was that he could initially focus on the internal members projected to be project team *leads*, which might include up to 10 individuals. His question was then "how much would be needed for this?" I told him I could probably help him arrange such training for about $10,000.

He hesitated in his response and then asked whether I would help in justifying spending of that amount. I replied "yes."

He responded, "Great, I'll set up a phone call between you and my wife. You can try to convince her that we don't need to take this year's annual winter vacation!" Needless to say, I didn't make the call.

## Developing a Practical Supplier Training Option

The point here is that facilitating an effective supplier development initiative without supplier personnel having basic manufacturing knowledge places a bigger burden on OEM supplier development resources, increasing the duration of the engagement and, thus, reducing their ability to promptly reach across an entire supply-base.

I investigated whether the needed training would be available from the state's technical college system, which, with 20 sites, had coverage across the entire state and whether the training would be consistent from campus to campus. My findings to each of these questions was "yes." I next posed the question of cost.

Because of the widespread reach of the community college system, most participating suppliers would have relatively local access to the training. This was an important factor since it would reduce lost time and the need to incur travel, lodging, and meal expenses.

When I investigated the cost of university training, I found that the technical colleges were the lowest-cost option. Despite this, their fees would still prevent participation in the training by some of the smaller suppliers. To fill this gap, it was apparent that outside funding would be needed to make technical college–based supplier training happen.

## Financing Supplier Training

In looking into tuition assistance, I found out that dollars *might* be available from my employer, depending on program structure. At a minimum I was told that participating suppliers would have to shoulder some of the cost; that is, there is no such thing as a *free lunch!*

## Federal Funding Support

At the time I was President of the Board of Directors of the state's Manufacturing Extension Partnership (MEP). The goal of this organization was to assist small- and medium-sized manufacturers become more competitive. The state's MEP received funding from the federal government, which was about one-third of the amount of the investment made by other stakeholders. The manufacturer would then have to only pay two-thirds of the cost of training. An additional portion of the training expense would be available if I could find other sources of funding, in effect further lowering the supplier's portion of the cost. So that's what I set out to do.

## State's Funding Support

I next scheduled an appointment with the state's Secretary of Commerce to pitch the idea, knowing that the state provided minimal funding support to its MEP. In spite of this, it did make the federal government a stakeholder in the program and, of course, made them provide a one-third match to other stakeholder funding. I went on to tell him of the funding commitment from my employer and the suppliers themselves and then asked if there was a possibility of getting additional funding for the state's MEP.

The Secretary liked the idea of funding training for the state's small- and medium-sized suppliers, that is, not large corporations. He also liked the idea of the training being conducted by the state's technical colleges, since the extra revenue generated by our program would reduce the need for state funding support of that system. He also explained that the current administration had prioritized helping the state's technical colleges increase their manufacturing outreach—with the goal of creating more manufacturing jobs within the state—and that our program very much aligned with this.

He listed three primary conditions for this to happen. First, the program could not be seen as taking work from available *free-market* private training providers. This was not a problem since we could show that they were not really interested in lower-revenue projects that cost under $3,000 per session.

Second, the state could not be seen as funding a particular corporation. To that point he insisted that I receive participation and financial commitment from at least five other large state-based OEMs. I had industry contacts from across the state and was able to meet this need through development of a multi-OEM member Supplier Training Consortium (STC).

Third, I would need to include one of my employer's primary competitors in the Consortium again, so it wouldn't appear that the state was favoring one corporation over another. I knew that this might be considered a bit *out-of-bounds* of my purview. However, I believed in the program enough that I decided to proceed without asking for permission. If need be, I would ask for forgiveness later!

I was able to convince a competitor to join the Consortium, which completed the necessary requirements for gaining state financial assistance.

## Supplier Funding Support

It was important to all outsider funding parties that participating suppliers partially fund their training. In my discussion with suppliers, I found that—for the most part—this would not be an issue as long as it was within their financial means.

In the end, the funding for training was split into four equal portions, that is, the federal government (funneled through the state's MEP); the state's Department of Commerce; the sponsoring OEMs, and the participating suppliers.

## My Employer's Involvement

Finally, I needed to go back to my employer, ask for forgiveness, and then ask for permission to proceed. Although some executives weren't especially happy that a competitor would benefit from the venture—and I took personal hits for putting the program together without first getting corporate permission—I eventually received forgiveness.

In fact, the company donated lobbying support with members of the state's Senate and House—which was needed since any funding would have to be taken from existing programs; that is, the state was operating under a budgetary *no-new-money* policy.

## Program Documentation

Preliminary to getting final state approval, the STC established organizational structure developing a Mission/Vision document, as follows, that would be used in getting support from the state's elected representation.

> *The Original Equipment Manufacturers making up the state's Supplier Training Consortium will provide a collaborative mechanism toward facilitating an integrated and results-oriented supplier training framework to gain competitive advantage for the state's small- and medium-sized manufacturers. The training will be provided by the state's technical colleges and guide them in curriculum selection and development. The state's Manufacturing Extension Partnership will provide overall program administration.*

*It will provide basic employee training to improve current work per-formance and to increase employee skills to make them a more valu-able resource. The training will also provide for continued supplier viability through improved competitiveness. Consortium members will generate an annual "curriculum of emphasis" based on their con-solidated performance expectations. Suppliers will be assisted by the OEM in training selection based on assessment of needs.*

## The Public and Supply Chain Announcements

The program was approved and judged to be a big enough deal that the state's governor traveled to my employer's out-of-state corporate head-quarters to participate in a *dog-and-pony show* with company's executives.

We next notified our Consortium's state-based suppliers about the program, asking if there was any interest on their part. The response was overwhelmingly "yes."

## Program Results

Over 5 years, 600 supplier employees attended the STC-sponsored train-ing. Based on the point that each supplier training would only have to have between 5 and 10 of their employees since they, in turn, return to their employer and roll-out training experience to all employees. Several thousand other supplier employees likely benefited from the outside training support.

At the end of the 5 years, the state decided to reallot STC funding; that is, if you already didn't know this, politicians can be fickle. At its end, the program met the goals outlined in the STC Mission/Vision.

The program had also met the goal of our being able to spread sup-plier development resources more quickly across our state-based suppli-ers, delivering financial benefit to them, and my employer sooner than would have been possible without the outside training support.

## Summary

It was recognized that increased supplier training would extend the scope of our existing supplier development resources. Although requiring sig-nificant work over the better part of a year, funding and a framework for implementing a program were put together to ensure such training was accessible to our suppliers that were in the state where our factory was located. The program was hugely successful, facilitating supplier improvement in quality and delivery performance as well as lowering ongoing supplier costs.

## Change Rating

*Revolutionary.* I had never heard of such a program being put together prior to our efforts, and haven't since.

## Lessons Learned

- Sometimes, it is better to go ahead with an idea— putting in place the needed infrastructure to implement a change—without first asking for permission. This may mean needing to hide an initiative in its early stages. It is easier to ask for forgiveness if you strongly believe what you put in place will be perceived to be in the best interests of your employer and that your proposal might not be approved up front.
- Don't fall into the trap that "if it were such a good idea, someone would already be doing it." I was told this by multiple of colleagues while trying to gain approval for the program. There's no reason to not position your employer as a leader of progressive supply management practices. This will require change.
- Selling a change internally when a Consortium participant is a competitor is possible. I made the case to my employer that our company would certainly outperform the competition on a *level-playing field*, knowing my employer's executives would be reluctant to dispute this point!
- Collaboration between OEMs and governmental resources can lead not only to increased positive financial impacts to OEMs and their suppliers but can also positively impact communities and even entire regions.

# CHAPTER 24

# Supplier Development Consortium

The experience gained in the development of the STC demonstrated that OEMs—and even their competitors—could collaborate on common goals and that suppliers were satisfied with the services provided by our state's MEP. This led to further consideration of how leveraging that organization's resources might result in a larger impact of an OEM's supplier management function.

To that point I began wondering whether the state's MEP could be used to do hands-on, boots-on-the-ground supplier development work, as well as whether any members from the STC would want to be part of such a program.

The hope here was that OEM endorsement of MEP services would convince a significant percentage of the Consortium's state-based suppliers to take advantage of them.

## Program Funding

Before trying to recruit Consortium members I felt that a general framework should be defined that would lay out a program framework, needs, and expected outcomes.

The first issue, of course, would be funding. The state had cut back the MEP funding that had been previously obtained for support of the STC. I knew that before going and requesting reinstatement of all or part of it, a good business case would need to be put together justifying it.

I anticipated that a wider breath of participation—rather than just one OEM—would be important to the state's Department of Commerce since it would dispel any criticism that state's monies were being spent in support of a single corporation.

To these two points, I contacted three of the OEMs that had participated in the STC and talked to them about my idea for a new, supplier development-focused Consortium. There was some interest, but they would need to see a solid business case justification. It wouldn't hurt that current suppliers to OEM members were spread evenly throughout the state, that is, had a presence in all political districts, and wouldn't hurt politically that the suppliers' spend was spread pretty evenly throughout the state.

I also understood that the financial impact the Consortium members had on the state through their annual spends(s)—for a total of $2.9 billion—would likely be an important element in getting state's financial support.

The three OEMs were primarily looking for evidence that MEP could effectively provide supplier development services and that the process they used to do so would be consistent across all their state-based suppliers.

I discussed this with the state's MEP, and we agreed on the following three parameters.

1. My supplier development group had developed an effective process for increasing a manufacturer's competitiveness through *true* lead-time reduction. We would formally document it and train MEP manufacturing resources in it. It is important to note that, for each engagement, parameters of the engagement were spelled out in a formal Memorandum of Understanding that, perhaps most importantly, the supplier *owned* all of the information and data from team efforts, meaning it could not be shared outside of the team without supplier permission.

2. MEP would provide onsite project support, while project oversight would be done under the auspices of existing OEM supplier development resources. As much as possible, this oversight would take place through mediums such as telephone and net meetings, which would help create a more efficient distribution OEM supplier development resources, expediting project outreach and helping keep initiative costs low.

3. In addition to actual *true* lead-time reduction, MEP would continue their strategy *of teaching-suppliers-to-fish*.

I next shared a sample of results delivered by our own supplier development group using this process.

## Increasing Overall Competitiveness Through *True* Lead-Time Reduction

As pointed out earlier in this book, reducing supplier *true* lead-time correlates with cost reduction, which aligned with the proven results of the Toyota Production System supplier development strategy. Our entire supplier development strategy and processes were based on this dictum, which meant identifying those waste-elimination actions that had the most potential toward reducing them and then prioritizing each for their being addressed.

## A Funding Hole

I then pointed out that, due to the similarity of manufacturing processes used to produce parts for our products, there might likely be cases of purchase overlap with individual suppliers. This ended up being the case in several instances and benefited such suppliers since it would reduce their assistance costs. It was also important because MEP's manufacturing staff was also limited. Because of this overlap, MEP would be able to benefit each OEM through a single-supplier engagement. For this reason, projects with these suppliers were also prioritized.

Despite the benefits outlined above, none of the Consortium members—including my employer—agreed to provide funding for the program. The issue was not that competitors participating would be part of the program, since none of the OEMs served the same or similar markets. It was rather that the companies weren't interested in financially supporting a program that would so directly benefit other companies. I disagreed with this approach but in this case knew I had to choose my battles. I accepted this position without debate.

## Back to the State's *Hat-in-Hand*

My next step was to go back to the state's Department of Commerce and justify the value of the project. To this point, the Consortium members had agreed to share our list of state-based suppliers, our annual spend(s) with them, and their locations. By the way, this type of OEM collaboration is almost unheard of.

The Department of Commerce was impressed by this data and doubled their MEP funding.

So, the program ended up being funded by suppliers, the state's Department of Commerce, and the federal government through their 33 percent match of other stakeholders' financial contributions.

## Program Results

Individual supplier's *true* lead-times were consistently cut by around 50 percent, reducing a significant amount of internal costs at the supplier end as well as at the OEM. For instance, when suppliers can more quickly respond to changes in schedule, less raw material stock is needed by an OEM. But there remained an overall supplier development gap.

All Consortium supplier companies had suppliers in other states. Even based on the results generated, the Federal MEP Office refused to formalize the process nationwide.

## Summary

Following up on the success of STC, an initiative was defined that justified the formation of a Supplier Development Consortium, with the MEP providing the bulk of the resources. Through a collaborative approach, a common supplier development strategy was adopted by Consortium members, and MEP personnel were trained to deliver the associated process. With the MEP doing the bulk of the onsite support work, OEMs were able to leverage their internal supplier development resources in support of out-of-state suppliers.

## Change Rating

*Revolutionary.* The Supplier Development Consortium created an example of how to increase the positive impact of a supplier development program by leveraging existing outside resources.

# Lessons Learned

- Success with previous initiatives will increase the ease of getting support for new ones. The success of the STC laid the groundwork for governmental and OEM support of a Supplier Development Consortium.
- Collaboration with other OEMs on similar objectives is possible if well-defined program boundaries are agreed upon. This collaboration can be beneficial in a number of ways, including creating a critical mass for gaining State support of initiatives.
- Infrastructure is needed to define the boundaries among OEM, MEP, and supplier participation.
- It was disappointing that the Federal MEP Office was unwilling to effect a change that based on actuals results would improve that organization's approach to supply chain support. OEM support of MEP system will not materialize if they are required to interact with individual state MEP Offices that do not deliver consistent processes and results across state lines. As a result, the MEP system also missed out on an opportunity to gain additional small- and medium-sized enterprises as customers as a result of OEMs' endorsement of such a program.

# CHAPTER 25

# Food Service Consolidation

As previously discussed, Imposter's primary strategy for negotiating was to gain and apply leverage in specific product categories by consolidating the spend of all Units in those categories. I had to agree that in some *cases* this might be a good strategy, but I was worried that it might be extended beyond those product categories—primarily commodities—where it made sense. I was right to worry because it soon became apparent that corporate purchasing wanted to consolidate *all* product categories into one buy, one of which was food service.

For this consolidation initiative, each factory received a letter from corporate stating that Unit food services were to be consolidated with a single national provider and that the details of our current annual spend needed to be submitted to them as a basis for planning. The letter was signed by Darth and the corporate Vice-President of Human Resources—probably to show that the initiative had expanded executive support—but left Unit Material Managers wondering why someone with no purchasing experience and/or authority would be a signatory.

My job was simple. My factory did not have a food service! That's right. Anyone wanting lunch needed to either brown-bag it or buy it out of a vending machine. Consequently, I didn't send in any data. I had none.

## Darth Being Darth

A week later, I got a phone call from Darth, who launched into a harangue about our factory not participating in the food service consolidation initiative and that this was unacceptable. I bided my time listening to him rant until he ran out of steam and then told him that our Unit didn't have a food service. He responded "oh" and hung up.

## Darth Being Darth—Redux

A week later, I received another phone call from Darth, in which he said he had learned we did have a food service. I was confused until he told me he was referring to our vending machines. As stated above, we did, but didn't consider them a food service. The bulk of the money spent on the snacks they contained was by our production employees, that is, union members. Our Unit Business Manager had negotiated an annual kick-back from our vending machine service and contributed it to the Union to help finance their annual summer picnic. I replied to Darth that this spend was controlled by our Unit Business Manager and I would connect with him to see how he wanted to handle it. Darth seemed pacified by this reply.

When I explained to our Unit Business Manager what corporate wanted to do with the vending machine kickback he replied "no," and with a small smile told me to communicate this to corporate. With my own small smile, I said "Perhaps that call would be more effective coming from you." He replied—with a bit of a smirk on his face—"I have every confidence that you can be effective in making the call yourself."

I called Darth and told him the news. He hung up on me without responding.

## Summary

Before any decision is made about whether to join a corporate initiative a Unit-focused business case should be put together either justifying participation or not, laying out the specific reasons for doing so. Our Unit's participation did not make logical sense; nor would it have had any real impact on the overall initiative, so we said "no."

## Change Rating

No change, hence no rating. The right thing here was to not partici-pate in corporate's consolidation intiative since it made no sense at our Unit.

## Lessons Learned

- Don't assume that corporate has done their homework prior to proposing enterprise-wide consolidation initiatives. To me, it was almost unbelievable that prior to launching the food service consolidation, they hadn't first learned that our Unit didn't have one.

- Don't allow yourself to be intimidated into participating in a change initiative when you are in the right but be prepared to explain the business case decision not to. In this case the decision was based on the relatively small vending machine spend that wouldn't detract much from initiative savings but would negatively influence the collaborative working relationship we had with our Unions if we took away the kickback funding.

# CHAPTER 26

# Centralization of Accounts Payable

## A Good Proposal

A proposal was made to centralize and standardize the company's Accounts Payable function within the Corporate Finance department. Payments to suppliers had previously been made at the Unit level, and there were differences between each Unit's payment processes which introduced room for error when a suppler sold to multiple Units within our company.

When I heard of this proposal I thought it was a great idea. In addition to the above, it would lessen staffing costs. It would also remove what was considered tangential work to Unit purchasing processes and allow individual Units to focus on more strategic tasks.

I was especially glad that the implementation plan would include a team comprised of Accounts Payable clerks from the company's larger factories, ours included. Based on the above I gave the initiative little further thought. I found later that this was a mistake.

The team came up with a common structure and process. Corporate rolled out the new approach, not feeling the need for Unit review/approval due to Unit employees having been on the process development team.

The structure and process were soon implemented, and it seemed to work well, at least initially.

## A Gap in Implementation and Process

Three months into the new, centralized approach, I heard from one of our suppliers. This supplier was our second highest spend and had closely collaborated over the years in cost reduction, product development, and other value-add activities.

He told me that his company—which invoiced us monthly—hadn't received payment in 2 months. This was a major problem since total Past Due payments had reached over $12 million. He asked me to look into and expedite payment. I apologized and said I'd look into it right away.

I contacted the supervisor of the centralized Accounts Payable department, reviewed the current issue, and asked if they had received the supplier's Request for Payment. He replied that they had but couldn't issue a check because the supplier hadn't correctly filled out the new payment submission form. I then asked if they had communicated this to the supplier and he answered "no."

I wasn't happy with this reply.

I explained to him that one of the things suppliers valued about selling to our company was that we always paid our bills on time. Delaying payment for such a minor issue would undercut supplier relationships. I then said I expected him to contact the supplier in question, train them how to fill out the new form, and pay them the Past Due amount immediately. He responded that it was a Unit's responsibility to work with their suppliers to ensure they knew how to fill out the new form. I asked him how we could be expected to do this when his department hadn't notified us that the supplier had submitted a payment request that had been rejected. He had no answer to this.

At this point I asked for the name and phone number of his manager.

## Further Stonewalling

I contacted his manager and described the previous discussion. I became more unhappy when he replied that he fully supported what his supervisor had said. Again, he posited that it was a Unit's responsibility to ensure that their suppliers adhered to corporate processes. He also said that if the corporate group would have to do so, they'd have to hire additional personnel, thus reducing the savings from the change.

I replied that this wasn't true since he could hire temps for a month or so to train suppliers on how to complete the new form as well as get supplier payments up-to-date. I added that when, in the future, new suppliers were added to our company's supply-base the payment submission form issue could be solved by having a detailed explanation about how to correctly fill it out on our corporation's Supplier Support Web Site.

He said, "We're not changing our position on this matter."

Our Unit's Business Manager was an old-timer who was well known and well respected across the company. He also knew just about all of the corporate managers and executives on a first-name basis, including the CFO who the Accounts Payable function reported to. I explained the situation to him, and he said let's talk to that manager again. He went on to say, "Let me do all of the talking and I'll take care of it."

## The Phone Call

My Unit Business Manager explained to the Accounts Payable Manager that I had updated him on the situation and that he thought I had suggested a reasonable fix. The manager gave him the same unsatisfactory response he had given me. The Unit Business Manager listened and then replied: "it appears we are at a loggers-head—it seems that the only solution might be that your CFO should be brought up-to-speed on this issue so he can tell us how to proceed. I'll give "Charley"—not his real name—a call and I think we'll be able to sort this out." The corporate Accounts Payable Manager recognized that by referring to the CFO on a first-name basis that our Unit Business Manager had a personal relationship with him and because of this would likely agree with our Unit's proposal.

Perhaps fearing that this would make him *look bad*, he replied—"that's not necessary—we'll proceed as you have suggested."

## Summary

Corporate had come up with a plan to centralize and take over the Accounts Payable function. In this case, centralization was a good idea. The implementation, however, showed there were glitches in how suppliers needed to fill out the new, standardized supplier Request for Payment form. Namely, there was a lack of supplier instruction and/or training on how to fill it out. Corporate's position was that it was a Unit's responsibility to deal with this, while Unit personnel felt the training issue could be more efficiently dealt with by the centralized office. In the end, corporate was induced to assume the responsibility.

## Change Rating

*Evolutionary*, since this was a good example about how Units can positively influence the setting up of centralized purchasing processes.

## Lessons Learn

- Corporate doesn't inherently have authority to make decisions without establishing a convincing argument and/or business case to justify their position. In this case, the approach they were advocating didn't pass the *smell*—common sense—test.
- In retrospect, don't have lower-level, tactical personnel represent Unit interests on corporate-led teams. This is especially true considering the corporate team leader will likely be a supervisor or manager—with more authority than the lower-level personnel—who, because of this, would not challenge the position on how to proceed. I, in fact, suspected that in this instance that the corporate team leader previously determined what the final outcome should be and had put clerical representatives on the team so he could later say that the Units had input to the team's output.
- Ideas are only ideas. Trying to implement change without a solid implementation plan is setting up an initiative for failure, good idea or not.
- Corporate functions not related to, or even having experience in managing suppliers, should respect the needs of purchasing when following up on glitches in their system.
- Finding the leverage to impose the purchasing position on such change may require support of executive management. In this case it did.

# CHAPTER 27

# Integration of Indirect Material and Services (IM&S)

Our Unit always seemed to be in the forefront of adopting new approaches to sourcing and purchasing. One example of this was when we were the first—and, at that time, the only—company Unit to use an IM&S Integrator.

IM&S Integrators combine the *buys* of their many clients to gain more leverage than individual companies alone could muster in negotiating with what are mostly commodity suppliers.

We had elected to work with a well-established Integrator and were half-way through the second year of a 3-year contract. They had delivered significantly lower pricing at the start of our relationship and had successfully met annual price reduction expectations. The fact was that operating as a single Unit within a single company we could not have obtained anywhere near the IM&S cost reduction we did working with our Integrator.

Corporate purchasing noticed that our factory was getting the lowest IM&S pricing in the enterprise, and one day I got a call from their IM&S manager. He wanted to know how we did it and, upon hearing how, proposed that the company use our approach as the overall company strategy for the purchase of IM&S.

I thought this was a great idea and explained that our buy would be available in little more than a year, and then could be added to overall company requirements, since we were only midway through our current 3-year contract. I also told him that at our upcoming annual review we'd let our Integrator know of company intentions and ask them initiate contact with his group.

I explained to him that it would take 6 months or so for other company Units to pull together and complete the groundwork necessary for them to participate in a corporate-wide RFQ. This meant that very soon after a new corporate contract came into effect, we could join it.

I was told that corporate wanted to gear up the initiative ASAP and that we'd have to break our contract once the company-wide implementation was rolled out. He also said he was sure the prep work needed by the other Units could be done within a couple of months.

The Uniform Commercial Code dictates that contracts cannot be broken as long as contractual terms are being met. This was the case with our Unit's IM&S contract.

Consequently, I told the corporate IM&S Manager that per commercial standards we could not ethically breach the contract. Hoping to find some middle ground, I went on to say that our Unit would be willing to put together an Integrator RFQ preparation class to facilitate and possibly shorten the prep time of the other Units. I thought this was a pretty good reply and figured they'd probably take me up on my offer. I was wrong.

## Corporate Interference

A couple of days later I was told by this same corporate IM&S Manager that not only would my Unit need to break the current contract, but that his group would travel to our Unit for the upcoming annual meeting with our supplier, which they'd conduct. I asked the reason for this and was told if we didn't have the wherewithal to break our contract with them, they'd do it for us and then begin negotiations immediately for an overall corporate contract.

I knew they hadn't had time to facilitate the necessary groundwork, told him so, and said they would not be involved in our meeting. He replied that he had Darth's backing for this plan and he would get him involved if I didn't go along with their proposal.

I was taken aback by what I considered an attempt as a unethical power grab and was admittedly a bit worked up after hearing what they wanted to do. I then said that I was not going to along go with his *proposal* and, as well, would gladly take a call from Darth.

After further consideration I also replied—in a friendly tone—that the drive from corporate headquarters to our factory—220 miles—was along a scenic route and, as the weather forecast was for a sunny day, they'd certainly enjoy the ride. I ended by saying, in a less friendly tone, that I was going to give their names to building security and that they would not be admitted into our Unit on the day of our meeting with the Integrator. He cursed at me and hung up.

In retrospect, the above may not have been the right approach to use in making my point, so decided it best to update my boss on the situation. He said I was doing the right thing. We didn't break the contract.

## Summary

Corporate purchasing had a consolidation proposal that—under the right conditions—made a lot of sense. It was a good strategy—which I supported—until I was told our Unit would have to break a contractual agreement with our current IM&S Integrator. We weren't willing to do that, which led to conflict between corporate and our Unit.

It is interesting to note that after our rejection of their proposal, corporate didn't proceed with a company-wide IM&S initiative.

I saw this as an indicator that corporate supply management was under extreme pressure from our company's executive group to deliver short-term savings, and once they saw that their IM&S proposal would take a year-and-a-half to come to completion, they turned their focus to other cost-reduction areas with more potential for short-term savings.

## Change Rating

No change, hence no rating. What had potentially been a highly *Evolutionary* change proposal—and impact—was lost. This was another case when corporate supply management went out-of-bounds in their actions.

## Lessons Learned

- Ethical purchasing personnel do not break existing contracts if the supplier has performed up to contract specifications. Word of such a move would undoubtedly quickly spread throughout the entire supply-base, causing supplier consternation, and threaten to weaken existing collaborative relationships.
- When it becomes clear that the other negotiating party isn't interested in finding middle ground and your business case is sound—stick to your position. Don't allow yourself to be bullied.
- What should have been an easy "win" for the corporation was not pursued. After all, the products purchased by the IM&S function are commodities that are—or should be—the bailiwick of corporate purchasing. It was clear that their proposal would have resulted in a financial boon for the overall company, but their lack of purpose showed that this was not their overall goal.

# CHAPTER 28

# An Interesting Meeting

A couple of hours after my phone call with the corporate IM&S Manager, my boss—our Unit's General Manager—came into my office and informed me that he had just received a phone call from Imposter. He had requested a meeting to discuss *issues* relating to the relationship between his corporate group and our Unit's purchasing function. The meeting was scheduled to take place on the following day.

Furthermore, he went on to say that Imposter, Darth, and the corporate IM&S manager would be taking the corporate jet up to our facility to meet with both him and our Divisional Vice-President. My boss told him he would also invite me to the meeting.

Our Unit's General Manager said he would brief the Division VP on the recent IM&S drama—which he expected to be the primary issue—and that I should expect a very difficult meeting the next day. He also advised me not to speak unless I was first spoken to.

## The Meeting's Real Focus

I pretty much knew the issue that corporate wanted to talk about was *me*.

The next day, I was sitting in our building's executive meeting room when the corporate group was ushered in. I smiled at them, but didn't say a word per my boss's recommendation. They looked at me with blank faces. It was pretty obvious they didn't want me there.

Imposter told my bosses that I hadn't cooperated with them on several key corporate purchased material cost-reduction initiatives, calling me a *rogue* operator. He went on to say I was apparently not interested in the financial health of the company as a whole, focusing only on my own Unit's interests. He then detailed each of the initiatives I had resisted, in which he said I had undercut them. They added that my actions and words relative to the recent IM&S spat were nonprofessional and unacceptable and that they had lost patience with me. Because of this they wanted me fired—or at a minimum—replaced.

The summary of perceived transgressions wasn't new to my management since I had always briefed them, justified the position I would take, and gotten their support on those positions.

In other words, Imposter VP of Purchasing was telling them things they already knew and had approved.

## Local Support

Our Unit Business Manager Divisional VP replied that he was glad that corporate had recognized that our Unit's approach to IM&S purchase was an organizational *best-practice*. He went onto say that he would support the implementing of it across the corporation after our contract expired. Furthermore, that we considered *our word* a gold standard as it was a basis of how our customers, employees, and suppliers evaluated us. And that we wouldn't break a supplier contract without good reason.

The Unit Business Manager then made two additional comments.

1. My role as a purchasing *change agent* was valued by our Unit as I had justified and implemented several changes that, in his mind, *were* in the best interests of both our Division and the company as a whole.
2. That our Division was not willing to take one step forward only to have to take two steps back, as he felt it would be by cancelling an existing contract. I wasn't sure what he meant by the *two-steps-back* comment.

He then asked me if I would be willing to drive the three back to the airport in our factory van. I said "yes" in response to his question, the only word I spoke during the meeting, I was thankful for his words—which pretty much ended the meeting. My job was safe.

## Follow-up

As you can imagine the trip to the airport was interesting. Imposter sat up in front with me, and we talked about sports, the weather, and so on. Darth and the Manager of corporate IM&S *stewed* in the backseat without saying a word. Darth was red-faced and it wasn't due to sunburn. The IM&S Manager looked crestfallen.

When I got back to the Unit, my boss stepped into my office and asked me whether the result of the meeting was to my satisfaction. I said "yes." He then said my participation in the meeting had surprised him. He could see I was confused, so he went on to elaborate—"I've never seen you be so quiet during a meeting. Despite the guidance I gave you about not speaking, I wasn't sure you could pull-it-off!"

That evening, I sat out on my front porch and smoked one of my best cigars and sipped on Jameson.

## Summary

Corporate purchasing wanted me fired and brought in big guns to try to accomplish that. They failed.

## Change Rating

*Evolutionary.* Corporate functions like to act as if they are the "all-knowing and powerful wizards" of the corporation. It only takes the "pulling aside of a curtain" to show they are not. Unit functional areas should maintain a strategic outlook and not follow corporate's lead when it is not justified. When the story of the event became known, I received congratulations from both colleagues and Divisional executives.

I had kept my job and never again got a pushback from this corporate purchasing administration.

## Lessons Learned

- This was an example of extreme bullying. It really does help to have kept your chain-of-command in the loop on possible future conflicts, that is, due to my *rogue* actions. If, in this instance, I hadn't, it is likely this meeting would have turned out differently.
- Later on in my career I didn't have such support. Despite this, I continued my in role as a *change agent*, although doing so

did lead to a lot of tension. The lesson here is—do what you think—and can show—is right. In the end, you'll feel better about sticking to your guns.

- Our corporate purchasing group put their own interests wanting to rush and take credit for the company's IM&S savings above all else. I didn't have much of a problem with the "take credit" part but wasn't willing to cancel a contract to facilitate a "rushed" initiative. Make sure their aims are visible so they can be seen and evaluated by others.

- It always pays to have a Plan B. Over the previous couple of years I had been regularly recruited for executive-level positions at other companies. At this time, I didn't want to move, but, if I had lost my job, I didn't think I'd have any trouble finding a new one.

# CHAPTER 29

# Cookie-Cutter Consultants

## Background

My favorite movie that touches on business consulting is *Office Space*—the movie with Jennifer Aniston and Ron Livingston. If you haven't already seen it, I'd highly recommend you do so. Those of you who know the movie will recall that the *two Bobs*, that is, Bob Slydell and Bob Porter, had been hired by Livingston's idiot boss, Bill Lumbergh, to reduce costs by *right-sizing* the company. Little did I know that later I would personally experience my own *two-Bob* experience.

## *Office Space* from a Personal Perspective

I've already described Irish's management strategy, that is, "if you're not with me you're against me." His second pronouncement was just as troubling.

He announced that by late February that our Unit would be expected to lay out a plan to reduce 15 percent of our salaried workforce by the end of the fiscal year, that is, October 31st.

Even if the headcount reduction was a good business decision, we were already one-third of the way through the year, which would leave us only 9 months for implementation, including figuring out how we would have to operate going forward with significantly fewer employees. Irish said he expected manpower cuts in every functional area.

This was not a good business decision, particularly for purchasing. I worked at my employer's third largest factory. Compared to purchasing department staffing across the corporation, our group had the highest efficiency, per corporate metrics of individual spend responsibility.

Added to that was during the previous fiscal year the Unit's purchasing had been *loosely* centralized within the Division—with an accompanying 15 percent headcount reduction—which the Units were still trying to deal with. Reducing another 15 percent from our headcount would essentially mean that over the last 12 months our department's workforce would have been cut by over a quarter. Irish's mandate was not justified either by our efficiency standing within the corporation or by the already implemented headcount cuts of the previous year.

What this meant to me—at least a first—was that Irish had made an arbitrary *cookie-cutter* decision not based on reality.

At the meeting where Irish first announced the *right-sizing*, our Unit's General Manager questioned the need laying off employees. He stated that with our factory's salaried employee workforce age demographics, a 15 percent reduction would happen within a year or two through retirement.

Irish replied that the headcount reduction would be expected by the end of the fiscal year., that is October 31. This proposal was denied.

Based on subsequent actions it was pretty clear that Irish now considered our General Manager "against him."

## The Process

Getting back to the movie, our Unit department managers were supposed to work with a consultancy firm that operated much like the two Bobs in *Office Space*. In addition to his 15 percent cookie-cutter reduction mandate, he had also hired a cookie-cutter-focused consultants to deliver it. Specifically, consultant personnel would monitor all salaried employee activities during the workday to determine how much of their time was spent *not* doing work tasks, according to their job descriptions—and, by this, show that there was wasted time that could be used to justify manpower reductions.

A study by the Association of Human Resources had recently shown that the average amount of productive time salaried employees worked over an 8-hour day was 5.3 hours. That left 2.7 hours of nonproductive—or according to the consultant—"waste" time. Based on an expectation of 8 hours of productivity a day, our consultant figured that one out of four employees weren't necessary, that is, 2.7 waste time $\times$ 3.1 employees = an 8-hour day, i.e. up to 25% of the current workforce.

Remember, our Unit's purchasing productivity metrics showed that our department did more with less number of employees than any other purchasing department in the corporation.

I guess I must have appeared dubious about the potential for head-count reduction in my department, which had caught the attention of the owner of the consulting firm. It especially caught his attention when his analyst's results showed that purchasing employee productivity exceeded the factory norm by quite a bit. It also showed that purchasing employees averaged over 1 hour of nonpaid overtime a day. The analyst's conclusion, then, was that a reduction in purchasing headcount made less sense than cuts in other Unit functional areas.

I reviewed these findings with the Unit's General Manager, and he agreed that cutting any personnel from the current purchasing headcount made no sense. But he also warned me that taking this stance could result in some sort of punitive action from Irish, who had made it expressly clear what he wanted.

## The Threat

Shortly after this, I was visited by the President and owner of the con-sulting firm. Without any prior notice, he walked into my office, closed the door, leaned over my desk, and asked me whether or not I was going to be a *team player*. He threatened to *torpedo* (his word) my relation-ship with Irish—who had engaged his firm—if I didn't agree to support the headcount reduction initiative. He also questioned my loyalty to my employer.

I told him to sit down and then calmly replied that he was out-of-line with his comments. First, the analysis of his own people showed no opportunity for a purchasing headcount reduction. Second, I had a record of 24 years of loyalty and positive financial impact on com-pany competitiveness and, if he doubted this, I'd give permission to Human Resources to give him access to my annual performance evaluations.

I didn't mention to him that Irish and I already had an antagonistic relationship, and I really didn't think he could damage it further. Finally,

I told him there would be no cuts in purchasing headcount and, if they tried to implement any without my agreement, I would go directly to the President of the Division who could then decide if cuts in purchasing were merited.

# The Initiative's Impact

There were several outcomes of the initiative.

- Overall salaried headcount was cut by 15 percent. In my opinion, this move was made less on available waste and more on the objective the consultancy was given. Sure, it makes a lot of sense to have a goal to shoot for. But it makes little sense for that goal to be, in effect, a guaranteed outcome. In my opinion, The over $1 million it cost to bring in a consultant was no more than to provide a justification for a predetermined outcome.
- There were no cuts in purchasing, which meant that higher cuts had to be made in other departments to make up the difference. Because of this, there was some animosity toward me from other department heads.
- It soon became apparent after the cuts were made that the Unit could not operate in an effective manner without the people who had lost their jobs. Irish's solution to this was to allow the Unit's General Manager to bring them back on, but only as temporary employees and at a much-reduced hourly compensation and no benefits.
- Our factory was in a rural area with very few opportunities for alternative employment, so most of the laid-off employees accepted the *temp* positions. This had a negative financial effect on not only the employees, but also the community and the entire region, with several businesses closing.
- Salaried employees' morale at this factory was all but destroyed. Going forward, we lost several of our top employees who found jobs with other companies. Irish did not allow the factory to replace these individuals.

- Irish got a substantial year-end bonus. I did some digging with a contact in Corporate HR, i.e., it's nice to have friends in high places. I discovered that one of Irish's performance goals was to cut headcount at our Unit by 15 percent before the end of the fiscal year.

## Summary

A decision was made based on personal—not business—reasons to cut 15 percent of the salaried workforce at our Unit. The Unit couldn't operate effectively at this level of headcount. This led to the employees who had been laid-off having to be brought back as *temps*. I was able to put together a business case justification that no headcount reductions should be made in purchasing.

## Change Rating

No change, hence no rating. While I protected the operation of my department, my Unit's efficiency and the region as a whole suffered greatly from the layoffs.

## Lessons Learned

- Irish had demonstrated many times *who-he-was*. It should not have been a surprise—and it wasn't to me—when he mandated a change for his own personal benefit. This displayed his lack of ethics and morality.
- When you find out how a person operates—in this case, a VP putting his own interests above that of one of the areas he has responsibility for and there is no way to block it—anticipate their actions and do what you can to prepare in advance to protect your area of responsibility. In this case, my business case justification was solid. In my experience, unfortunately, lack of ethics is not rare in Corporate America.

- If I had gone along with the 15 percent reduction, it would have negatively affected the performance of our group. Probably more importantly, I would have lost some of the trust that my people had in me.

Leaders need the trust of their employees to both maximize their current performance and accept beneficial changes to departmental strategies and processes. In other words, you cannot be a leader and/or *change agent* without the support of your employees.

# CHAPTER 30

# Executive Guidance on Meals

At one point in my career, I worked for a director who was *budget-conscious* to an extreme. This meant not only that he focused on *spending to budget*, which can be a good thing, but also in lowering his departmental budget year to year, gaining positive executive-level visibility. Why? Because he felt this would demonstrate to his superiors that he had a strong focus on cost reduction, even when the cost avoidance would have a negative influence on employee morale, as well as regard for his leadership.

Along these lines—at most staff meetings—he would preach that meals paid for by the company shouldn't cost more than the meals you'd eat at home. So, it appears that at least in his mind that Subway was a good alternative for either lunches or dinners.

## Do What I Say, Not What I Do

The Director had come from another Division within the company, and, while talking to one of his former direct reports, I asked if he had also emphasized minimizing meal expense there. He smiled and said, "It depends on what you mean by minimizing." When I asked him what he meant by this, he asked me, "Do you consider dining at Ruth Chris minimizing?" When I replied "no" and asked what he was implying. He said that the person who was now my Director had once treated his staff to a dinner at Ruth Chris on the company's dime, which, if you don't already know, is one of the most expensive restaurant chains around!

I had finally had my fill of the Director's preaching on this subject, so, at one of his staff meetings, raised my hand and asked if this meant not eating at establishments such as Ruth Chris. He said "yes," but I was sure he knew where I was going with this. I then asked if he had ever had business meals at a Ruth Chris restaurant and, with a red face, he admitted he had in his previous position. He then went on to say that he eventually came to understand he had made a mistake.

My response was something to the effect that I was sure the dinner had been appropriate, given the situation, which did not at all reflect my opinion on the subject. He didn't reply, but also never again brought up the topic of meal expense at future staff meetings.

But I knew that probably wasn't the end of it. I had made a point but figured I would pay for it eventually. I was right and below I'll lay out two cases that show what I mean by this.

## Dinner with My Wife

While reporting to this Director, I was transferred from the Unit I had spent 19 years at to our new Divisional headquarters. This was a major unsettling to my family and was, in my mind, unnecessary. Nevertheless, I was given 2 weeks' notice to accept the move or be separated from the company, so with 26 years of service on the line I accepted it.

Upon arriving at our new location, I was a bit surprised by my boss when he invited me and my wife out for a "welcome" dinner at a nice area restaurant. The discussion was pleasant enough—probably since my wife was there—but I was deeply surprised (and upset) when at the end of the meal two checks were brought out for payment. The first was for my boss and me, which he paid for. The second was for my wife's meal, which was given to me to pay. I asked my boss for an explanation, and he replied something to the effect that since my wife was not an employee, he could not pay for her meal out of the departmental budget. Some welcome.

## Supplier Development Leadership Dinner

As the company's supplier development Process Owner, it was my responsibility to both coordinate standardizing processes between Divisions and have each Division share engagements they had successfully conducted that reduced supplier cost. This was before the advent of online meetings and, consequently, face-to-race meetings were the primary approach for accomplishing this.

EXECUTIVE GUIDANCE ON MEALS   167

The meetings usually were several days in length, and, while participants were generally responsible for their own evening meals, after the
last day of the conference we congregated for a celebration at a relatively
upscale—not at the Ruth Chris level—restaurant. A common practice at
restaurants when serving larger groups is to consolidate the end-of-meal
bill and that was the case here. Since I had set up the meeting, I took care
of the total meal expense, which, with 14 participants (and tip), came out
to about $1,500 dollars.

When my boss saw this, he was upset. He said he shouldn't have to
pay for employee meals when they were outside of our Division.

Consolidating bills for group meals was a generally accepted practice
in our company. It so happened that my widowed mother lived near
our corporate headquarters. When visiting corporate I would stay with
her—avoiding hotel expense—and eat meals at her house—or take her
out to dinner—without charging the company for the either the lodging
or the meal.

## A Reality Check

I later learned the Director had complained about this to one of my own
employees. This employee pointed the above arrangement out to the Director and said that it showed I was budget-conscious. After all, I had only
done what was considered acceptable practice within the company. The
Director seemed mollified by this explanation, but I suspected it was because if he were to take it "up the ladder" he felt there was a good chance
his hierarchy would have sided with me.

## Summary

Our Division's Director of Purchasing harped continually at staff meetings to reduce company meals expenses. When it was pointed out to him
that this was a bit like "Do as I say, not as I do," he backed off. He also
wasn't interested in following corporate practice if he could make it appear that he was aggressively managing his budget, even at the expense of
one of his own employee's reputation.

He didn't realize that due to actions such as those described here, he not had not only lost my trust but also, when people heard about his actions toward me, the trust of the department.

## Change Rating

*Incremental*, but personally important.

## Lessons Learned

- You don't have to put up with bullying from your boss if you can show he has acted in the same manner he was criticizing you for, especially if you can show you were acting within the parameters of company policy.
- When my boss traveled, he stayed in expensive hotels and ate meals at upscale restaurants. "Do as I say, not as I do" is both obvious and undercut his standing within the Division's purchasing group. Do not operate in this manner if you expect to have the support of your employees.
- As stated throughout this book, being ethical is important on an individual basis; that is, if you are unethical and don't have regrets being so, you are essentially working for compensation rather than for the good of your employer.

# CHAPTER 31

# Executive Guidance on Moving Expenses

Later in my career, due to Irish's ongoing antagonistic treatment of me, I started positioning myself for a move to another organization within the company. A transfer eventually came to fruition when I was offered a position at our corporate headquarters.

My current job was on the East Coast of the United States. My transfer would be to the Midwest. My wife and I also had a home on the West Coast, and she indicated that, rather than living in the Midwest, she preferred to live at our West Coast location. This seemed somewhat of a possibility since at that time I had enough vacation that—combined with company holidays—I could go home for a week every month-and-a-half, or so. I had also accrued over 100 days of unused vacation that I could also access as needed.

At that time my employer paid for relocation expenses, including financial assistance in purchasing a new home and the actual moving of a personal belongings. I went to Corporate HR and asked if it would be possible for the company to pay the cost of moving our belongings to the area of corporate headquarters and then have me pay for the expense of having them delivered to where my wife wanted to live. I also explained that I wouldn't be needing the offered home purchase financial assistance since my mother lived near corporate headquarters and I was planning to stay with her.

I was given the OK for this plan by Corporate HR and thought this would be the end of it. It wasn't.

## Budget—and Not Personnel—Concerns

My boss asked me to come into the office one day and told me he would not approve paying for the transfer of our personnel belongings. Not just from the Midwest to West Coast (which I hadn't anticipated) but, overall, including from my current location to the Midwest.

I asked for an explanation, and he replied that it was obvious that I was planning to leave the company after my 30-year anniversary date—which was only 2 years away—and he didn't think it appropriate for the company to provide funds to facilitate my early retirement from the company.

Of course, he was attempting to retain funds that would otherwise come out of his Divisional purchasing budget.

I said that whether this was true or not, I always had the option of having them delivered to my mom's house at the company's expense and then have them reloaded onto the moving van and transported to the West Coast at my expense. He suggested I do just that that. I replied, *"because that it would make no sense."* I walked out of the office saying, as I left, that if he wanted to discuss the matter further, he should connect with Corporate HR, which had approved the plan.

## Summary

My boss tried to bully me by denying me routine company relocation benefits. This demonstrated a lot of things about his ethics, or lack thereof, since he seemed to be more concerned about his departmental budget than supporting a long-time, high-performing employee. Knowing "who-he-was" I had previously gotten Corporate HR approval for my relocation plan. After telling him this, he dropped the subject. Any respect I had previously had for him was gone due to the unfair financial burden he had tried to impose on me, which in my mind was unethical.

## Change Rating

*Incremental*, but personally important.

## Lessons Learned:

- Again, when a person demonstrates who they are, believe them.
- Some managers are more interested in making their own performance look good rather than taking care of their employees. My boss reported through Engineering to Irish and

probably either held him up as a role model or just wanted to impress him with how ruthlessly he managed his departmental budget. Here again is an example of a lack of ethics.

- Don't allow yourself to be bullied. It only leads to more bullying. In this case, I was responsible for gaining the approval for moving expenses and gotten an OK for my relocation plan. This type of organizational approval is very difficult to override.
- If you have options, don't put up with working for a manager who acts unethically. If you accept such actions, know that at some point that manager will again treat you in an unethical manner.

# CHAPTER 32

# Collaboration from a Personal Perspective

Earlier in my career I had proposed a three-supplier Proof-of-Concept pilot based on *true* lead-time reduction as its guiding principle but had no resources to implement them. I was told by my Unit's General Manager that without financial justification, he wouldn't give approval to add to the purchasing department headcount. This represented a bit of a conundrum. I couldn't provide the financial justification he had asked for without resources to run my pilot.

I looked at my own department budget and found that I could afford to "hire" enough corporate industrial engineers on a consulting basis to conduct the pilot, i.e. this was at a time when some amount of discretionary funding was allowed in a manager's budget. I then started looking for suppliers to be the test cases.

I decided to focus on three of our most underperforming suppliers since I suspected it we would have more waste reduction opportunities there than with a random sample.

## One of the Supplier Development Pilot Participants

Our factory had one supplier that, although they had significant design and processing advantage over their competition, had poor On-time Delivery performance. In fact, it had reached the point where our schedulers were ordering parts from them 2 weeks ahead of time to ensure they would be delivered in time for production. We also had to hold a relatively large stock of raw material of their parts for use when they couldn't respond to short-fuse orders in less than 2 weeks.

I ended up informing the owner of the company that I had made the decision they would not be assigned new business until their delivery issues were addressed. He replied that they were aware of their poor On-time Delivery performance and, in fact, had plans to address it shortly. He asked for a one-on-one meeting to explain these plans, so I visited him at his factory for that purpose.

## The Wrong Approach

At the beginning of the meeting, he indicated that he knew that they had difficulty in managing finished goods inventory and that this led to their not being able to locate batches that had already been run. This was the reason they weren't shipped on time. We purchased a high volume of over a dozen part numbers from them. Added to this, the product they manufactured was common for all competitors with minimal differences in design. So, they literally had inventory of dozens of part numbers that looked relatively similar. The only *saving grace*—if you can call it that— was that our competitors also had to deal with this supplier's On-time Delivery issues, so our experience didn't provide them with a competitive advantage!

The owner explained that they would be purchasing an electronically operated automated rack inventory system. I asked what it would cost, and he replied $500,000. This might not seem like much today, but in 1996 it represented a major capital investment, especially for a company that was relatively small in size.

Also, if they went forward with their plan, I was pretty sure this would place pressure on his company to increase our pricing. I didn't bring the issue up at the time.

## Supplier Development Invitation

I mentioned to him that we were looking to staff a supplier development function and, therefore, could offer him industrial engineering support that would probably forego his need to invest in the inventory control system. He asked, "How much would these services cost?" I replied, "They would be provided at no charge, but we'd want a portion of any cost reduction." He then asked who would quantify the cost reductions, and I told him that his organization would. He was a bit surprised by these terms and readily agreed to the offer.

We started our assessment of his shop the next week. First, understand, we weren't only reviewing the production of our own parts. Rather, we knew that in order for a supplier to capture meaningful savings—and grant us meaningful price reductions—we would have to address the processing of all of the parts they produced, including those for our competitors.

In discussing this with the owner, I said that I wouldn't tell our competitors of any cost reduction at his factory, and it would be up to him to decide whether to offer them one. He said, "fat chance," and I knew our engagement in his factory had the potential to give us a quantifiable competitive advantage, cost-wise.

## The Supplier Development Engagement

We soon found that their current average *true* lead-time was 14-days and that was for parts that only required three steps of processing. This, of course, was a result of completed batches and work-in-progress (WIP) being stacked somewhat haphazardly around their factory. We were able to address this by streamlining processing such that *true* lead-times were reduced to 2 days. For the most part, this eliminated their late delivery problems. It also eliminated the need for the supplier to make a $500,000 capital investment.

## Quantifiable Results

We split a cost reduction of over 15 percent. We had similar results from the other two suppliers in our pilot, and this helped justify having a full-time supplier development function at my Unit.

At our Division's annual supplier conference, the owner of the first supplier we had worked with spoke to the entire supply-base about his interaction with our supplier development group. He said our supplier development support was different from what they had likely experienced or heard about and told of the specifics of the savings the project had delivered.

## Additional Project Benefits

With this project, we had not only delivered on what we had said we would but had also developed a highly collaborative relationship with the supplier going forward. For instance, further work with their design and manufacturing functions eliminated one of the three processes used in the manufacture of their parts—including setup—by integrating a machining process with the part's prior stamping operation.

## Irish Shares His Intention to Fire Me

Fast forward 18 years. As previously discussed, Irish seemed to have it in for me, not based on poor performance but, instead, for personal reasons; that is, he didn't see me as a team player. The supplier with whom we had conducted our initial Proof-of-Concept supplier development work had opened a factory located near our Division's engineering headquarters. Irish worked out of this facility and knew the owner of the supplier since I had previously introduced the two.

Irish, it seemed, liked to rub elbows with men of accomplishment—probably hoping that some of their success would rub off on him. To this point, he set up a recurring dinner with the owner of the supplier organization described above during his monthly visit to his new factory.

At one such dinner, Irish said something to the effect of "I know you have a high regard for Paul Ericksen, but I'm going to have to let him go." The supplier's owner reply went something along the lines of "You need to do what you think is best for your business, but, if you fire Paul, we can't be friends." I heard of this whole interaction from the supplier's Manufacturing Manager and later confirmed it.

I wasn't fired. Talk about the benefits of customer–supplier collaboration!

I'm pretty sure that without the relationship I had built with this guy and his company, I would have been out of a job.

It was also interesting to me that Irish would share his intention to fire an employee with someone outside of the company, which I regarded as a unprofessional act. Luckily for me, though, he had.

## Summary

A successful supplier development project satisfactorily addressed a supplier's delivery performance problem and set the stage for years of collaborative success, which over time contributed to their becoming a World-Class manufacturer.

A few years after I retired, in fact, this manufacturer was named as my former employer's overall Supplier-of-the-Year.

Personal relationships are important in business. They result in trust and respect. One outcome of the relationship between our factory and this supplier—which included one between me and the supplier's owner—ended up with this supplier standing up for me.

## Change Rating

*Revolutionary.* This verified that our supply collaboration strategy was effective and, at the same time, saved my job. I've never heard of a similar story.

## Lessons Learned

- Sometimes good deeds do go rewarded. There's no doubt that if I had worked with this supplier in a win-lose manner, he wouldn't have taken the position he did with Irish.

# CHAPTER 33

# The Fuel Gauge Dilemma

The Division I spent the bulk of my working career for once had a vision of dominating the market we served, and, over time, we did. In 1984, the Division consisted of a *single* factory and sold $250,000 worth of products. Fast forward to 2006, when the Division's *four* factories sold products worth $6 billion.

Our strategy to achieve this had been three-fold. First, to concentrate on expanding our product line to gain a larger cross-section of customers. Second, to significantly update or replace products every 3 years to ensure that we continued to meet the increasing customer expectations. Finally, we would manufacture and sell product to our competition based on products we already manufactured to fill gaps in their product offerings. The end goal was to manufacture the bulk of lawn and garden products, even if they were sold under a different brand name.

Of course, a consequence of this would be that our products as well as products we produced for other manufactures would be in competition. While the first two of the above strategies were successful, the third was not.

## A Failed Strategy

Our first—and last—experience as a manufacturer of competitor products was to make minor adjustments to one of our *industry best* products and then paint them in the customer's color scheme. They would sell these products through their own distribution network, either at a price higher than ours—to keep their profitability acceptable—or accept a lower margin. How could we lose?

Potential customers, however, soon came to realize that our and the competitor's products were essentially the same. This knowledge soon spread like wildfire throughout the industry and had a significantly negative impact on the competitive company's sales. Why? Because there was very little differentiation between them and customers generally want to buy *the real McCoy.*

As a result, after the first year of the arrangement, our outside purchased product (OPP) customer had only sold about half of their anticipated sales, leaving them with a lot of finished product inventory. At this point they said they wouldn't be buying additional machines unless we could provide significant differentiation between the two versions of the machine.

## A Dumb Proposal

Product design changes had to be approved by a committee comprised of design and marketing personnel. Once approved, the change(s) were expected to be implemented without opposition. Some marketing *genius* (I hope you note the sarcasm in my use of the term) decided that the needed product differentiation could be provided by adding a fuel gauge to the product we were selling to the competitor—ours didn't have one.

When I heard about this, I was extremely dubious that the proposed fix would meaningfully address the differentiation issue. And it would likely negatively impact the sales of a significant amount of finished product that had been built without the fuel gauge that the OEM customer had already purchased and had in stock.

## Exposing the Reality of the Proposal

I had the authority to either approve or disapprove the costs associated with new and/or revised tooling. The adding of a fuel gauge would require a significant change to the molding tool used to integrate a fuel gauge to the control panel as well as to the fuel tank itself. The cost would be $20,000, or so, each. Remember, this was in the early 2000s when $40,000 was considered a significant expenditure for a feature that would provide minimum value. In addition, any customers that bought the competitor's product because of the fuel gauge update would likely represent at least some lost sales to us.

As I said above, I had little faith that the proposed design change would make any significant difference in our competitor's future sales of the product. This would mean, should the relationship end, we would have a $40,000 sunk investment unless *we* added the fuel gauge to *our* product, which would mean a price increase or reduction in margins, neither of which marketing would accept.

## The Outcome

To make a long story short, I ended up not approving the tooling change and, because of this the issue became a point of extreme controversy. I was approached by the committee's marketing representative who told me that I had no choice in the matter, per Unit policy. I again refused. He left my office saying that I had not heard the last of this issue.

Shortly thereafter, my Unit's General Manager came into my office and closed the door, usually not a good sign. He said that the Division's Marketing VP had just telephoned him and asked him to order me to approve the tooling changes or "put someone in the job that will."

I asked my boss if he was familiar with the details of the circumstance that were driving the need for the tooling changes. He said he wasn't, so I filled him in. He was silent for a period, and I could tell he was thinking. He went on to say:

> *I am disappointed—not in you—but with the product change committee.*

He went on to say that he agreed with me on all counts and that he would "take care of it."

I then asked him if this meant I wouldn't be replaced and he replied, "No, not at this time, but you always need to keep in mind that I have the option to do so!" He was smiling as he said it, so I didn't give it much thought going forward.

## Summary

We became a supplier to a competitor, selling a version of one of our products already in our product lineup. The competitor felt that this was the lowest-cost way to fill out their product offerings.

We started manufacturing the competitor's version of the product; however, since there was little differentiation between our product and the one being sold to them, demand for their product was low.

A design change that would hopefully differentiate the two products was approved by the *design approval committee*. I was dubious it would provide the needed differentiation. It would also require spending to revise two tools.

I controlled the budget for purchased tooling and, without my approval, the proposed revisions could not take place. I did not approve it, and this led to a conflict between marketing and purchasing.

## Change Rating

*Evolutionary.* It created a precedent going forward for better oversight of decisions coming out of the product design committee. In addition, the change created an example of the benefits of giving purchasing a seat at the table in making design-revision related decisions.

## Lessons Learned

- If something doesn't seem to pass the *smell test*, feel free to challenge it, even if the underlying decision was made outside of your area of responsibility.
- Be prepared for backlash to your challenge. Because of this make sure you have solid argument for taking your position.
- If you strongly believe in your concern, don't allow yourself to be bullied by someone threatening to take the issue *up the ladder.*

# CHAPTER 34

# Promoting One's Department's Performance at the Expense of Another's

Policies are written to provide *guidelines of practice*. Specifically, they define predetermined sets of behavior for addressing scenarios that could occur during the normal course of doing business. In addition to providing guidance, however, they also function as a vital means of defining activities between functional areas—such as product design and purchasing—and between organizations, such as OEMs and their suppliers.

Our Division had a policy that defined timing guidelines for implementing design changes based on the current level of manufacturing *stress*. Demand seasonality was a big issue for our factory and suppliers, with up to two-thirds of annual sales occurring over only a quarter or so of the calendar year. For the most part, since we built to demand, there were times of very high production—where manufacturing stress was rampant—as well as times where production was either very low or was, in fact, stopped, leading to little or no stress.

During a period of high manufacturing stress the impact of the slightest production *hiccup* is magnified. Consequently, business risk associated with product design changes varied greatly depending on whether a factory is experiencing peak production or not. This is where a policy can play an important role. The design change policy at our Division included the following guidelines:

- Design changes required to address safety issues would be implemented immediately.
- Design changes that would significantly increase customer perceived product value would be implemented as soon as

practically possible, with the term *practically* assuming
common-sense timing.
- All other design changes—including those that would lead
  to purchased part–price reduction—would be made during a
  non–peak production period.

This policy had been set up with a goal of avoiding the higher risk of
quality problems and/or productivity loss during a period when both our
manufacturing facility and the manufacturing facilities of our suppliers
were under their greatest pressure.

## Not Adhering to the Design Change Policy

During one such peak production period, I received a design change request on a purchased part. Since the change was not related to product
safety or improved value I rejected the request for immediate implementation. Instead, I scheduled it for an upcoming production lull. This was
an organization in which purchasing reported up through Product Engineering, and the next morning the VP of Product Engineering stepped
into my office and closed the door.

He asked me why I was delaying the implementation of a design
change originating from his department. I cited the product change policy. He replied that the change would yield about $0.13 savings per part
and that over the next 6-week peak production period over 100,000 units
would be manufactured, yielding a total savings of $13,000.

I explained about the high risk of production-related problems, which
would be very high if they occurred, where the costs associated with addressing them could significantly outweigh a $13,000 in savings.

This was an explanation he didn't want to hear. As he walked out of
my office his last words to me were—"Just manage it or, if you don't think
you can, I'll find someone who will!" I got the message and approved the
immediate implementation of the design change.

## Following Orders

My next step was to *just manage it*. I called the supplier we bought the
part from to give them a heads-up on what was coming and asked if there

was anything I could do to help them mediate their manufacturing risk. His reply was along the following lines:

- Their normal operation was a 5-day, 2-shift week.
- To support the coming production peak, they would have to ramp up to a 6-day, 3-shift schedule, with the extra manpower to be hired through temporary employment agencies.

Because the change was to be implemented with virtually no opportunity to prepare the current employees for the change—and train the new employees—he felt that successful implementation of the change would require intensive supervisory oversight, something his company didn't have the means to provide. He asked if we could send in supplier development engineers to assist supervising production during the off-shifts—those with the most temporary employees—which I agreed to do.

## Remedial Actions and Their Associated Costs

The out-of-pocket costs of providing this supplier development support were approximately $60,000 for things such as airline tickets, car rentals, lodging, and meals, since we would need to have 2 men on 2 shifts, 6 days a week.

With these thrown in, the cost to "manage" the immediate implementation of the design change—remember, it was for a $13,000 savings—overshadowed the savings by just under $50,000.

The supplier development support was, in fact, needed since through our supervision several instances of what would have been significant production foul-ups were prevented, which themselves would have led to rework and delays. Additionally, a few of them—if they had not been caught—would likely have required product field modification, a very expensive activity.

## A Selfish Decision

Being naturally curious I did a little nosing around afterward to try to figure out *the rest of the story.* Our peak production period coincided with the end of a financial quarter, and Product Engineering had quarterly cost-reduction goals that figured prominently in evaluation of their performance. The $13,000 savings allowed them to achieve their current quarterly cost-reduction goal.

## Summary

I was ordered to act outside the lines of a time-tested policy, which was designed to reduce operational and financial risks. I was threatened with replacement if I didn't do so. Consequently, I felt I was in no position to refuse the *request*. Fortunately, I had the resources available such that I was able to put together and implement a plan to mediate the risk. If I hadn't had the resources, the minor cost savings would have led to a significant financial loss.

## Change Rating

No change, hence, no rating.

## Lessons Learned

- Properly crafted policies can be important in guiding activity. Deviating from a policy should require visible risk and financial justifications.
- Performance metrics—particularly those related to savings—need to be cross-functionally balanced, or they run the risk of causing competition between functional areas to meet individual department saving's goals, which can lead to inter-departmental win-lose results.
- Executives aren't above putting their personnel and/or department needs above company benefit—as if anyone really doubted this.

Note: Afterward I felt I had let my employer down. More importantly I felt guilty about my actions in this snafu. I still think there must have been something I could have done to prevent this goat rodeo from happening—perhaps by "rain-bowing" my boss and laying out the cost comparison up the ladder for a final decision about whether to proceed with the change or not.

# CHAPTER 35

# The Con Artist

My favorite purchasing job was that of Materials Manager. Why? Because—prior to Imposter becoming the Vice-President of Purchasing—the job was pretty much independent of either corporate or Divisional interference in the setting of effective *local* purchasing strategies, policies, and practices.

One of my Materials Manager colleagues and I had, over time, developed a close friendship. Later he was offered—and accepted—a Materials Manager position at a larger factory.

My friend's replacement was recruited from outside the company, having been hired by a new factory manager who had also recently been recruited from the outside. While I believed there were plenty of good internal candidates for the Materials Manager position, I understood the desire to bring into our company people with new ideas and insights.

## A Red Flag

Shortly after his hiring—in an interview with an internal company publication—the replacement stated that his primary goal was to bring a higher level of "professionalism" to the factory's purchasing function. This had not only offended my friend but had also raised a red flag in my mind about the new guy, especially since that factory's supply-base had been performing above the company norm in most areas.

Although the factory where I was Materials Manager lagged behind other factories in annual material price reduction, it had the best On-time Delivery, Quality, and largest *Employee Span of Control* in the corporation. During my tenure we had set up purchasing strategies, policies, and practices in a sustainable way such that if I might be moved to a position outside the factory, the factory would continue to set the corporate standard in these areas.

I was a bit surprised that shortly after the new Materials Manager assumed his position, his factory's supplier On-time Delivery and Quality improved substantially such that *they* now were the best in the corporation. The factory's price reduction performance had also improved.

## Further Questionable Advancement

Later I was offered and accepted a job at Division headquarters. A year-and-a-half later, my replacement as Materials Manager—at the factory where I had been located—retired and was succeeded by the same guy who had previously backfilled my friend. His promotion was from a small factory to the third largest in our corporation, and many people wondered why he had been given such an increase in responsibility so quickly.

I didn't wonder, however, as the factory manager who had initially hired him had—in the meantime—become the company's Vice-President of Purchasing. In other words, I suspected the new VP's hand in the promotion, since it would both help cement that idea that he had hired a high-potential individual and the new VP would also now have someone who would be beholden to him.

The replacement at his previous factory wouldn't be available for about 6 months and, due to my previous Materials Manager experience, I was tasked with temporarily filling in there during that interval. I was excited as I had never expected to get a chance to be in my favorite position again.

## Discovering a Deception

Upon arriving at the factory, however, I was surprised to see a couple of hundred units of product sitting in the rework yard. When I asked about this my guide replied that they were units missing purchased parts. The equipment had been partially assembled and would be completed upon receipt of them.

This didn't sync with the factory's purchased parts On-time Delivery metrics. It also ran against a corporate mandate not to build equipment that would need rework due to a lack of purchased parts, whether from late deliveries or quality issues.

I started digging into this situation but was stonewalled by purchasing department personnel in getting an explanation for the discrepancy. I decided that the best way to get to the root of the issue was to have a private conversation with the department's senior person. And I decided the best place to do it would be at a local bar.

After several steins of beer I brought up the question about how the factory's supplier On-time Delivery performance could be so high while a significant number of units were in the rework yard waiting for delivery of purchased parts. I also asked about how the performance had risen so quickly.

The guy's explanation was surprising and made me so angry that I internally cursed the man who had—in replacing my friend—promised a "more professional purchasing function." He explained the mystery behind the factory's high-purchased part On-time Delivery improvement. He also went on to say departmental employees were embarrassed by their associated actions, which is why they had been hesitant in talking to me about them.

It turned out that department personnel had been instructed by their Materials Manager that if more than one part was late, only the first part would be reported as late. The justification for this was the others were not *actually* late since they were not the initial part that was required to complete the product assembly! And if that first part was delivered, only the second late part would be considered late in the factory's On-time Delivery computation, and so on.

Furthermore, I found that the bulk of the late parts in question had recently been resourced to overseas suppliers, an initiative that the new Materials Manager had accelerated in a quest for better factory-purchased part-price reduction performance. It was obvious—at least to me—that the assessment of the overseas suppliers had primarily focused on price to the disregard of everything else.

## An Appropriate Response

In my mind what I had uncovered was unethical. While this type of behavior may have been acceptable at the guy's previous employer—I highly doubted this—it would certainly not fit into the culture of my employer. Consequently, I knew I could not let it stand.

I met with the factory manager and described what I had found. He seemed surprised but asked me to "just take care of correcting the practice." I replied that I would immediately revise it to what was standard practice in the company but felt the issue required further follow-up. He disagreed, implying that while this might be reasonable on an individual basis, it would be to the greater good for both the factory and corporation that what had happened be swept *under the rug*.

It was clear that I had been presented with a moral decision. I could either go along with the cover-up or reveal what had occurred with the knowledge that doing so would undercut my relationship with the VP of Purchasing and the factory manager. In the end, though, I felt that the risk of the individual continuing to operate in this way in the future was high enough that the issue should be moved up the ladder.

I knew that bringing up what I had uncovered could only be effectively presented to executive management with fact-based data to back it up. I went about analyzing the factory's Last-12-Month delivery and price reduction performance and was able to show that there was a direct correlation between late deliveries and the improved purchased material cost-reduction. This was real data that could not be disputed.

I presented my findings to the Division's Purchasing Director since although my regular job was at corporate and the VP of Purchasing was now at the top of my formal reporting structure, in my interim position I had been given an informal reporting relationship at the Divisional level.

## The Resulting Impact

The nefarious acts of this person never became popularly known but I had the feeling that appropriate action would eventually be taken. I wasn't wrong. A couple of months later he was fired. But that was not the end of the story.

After my temporary factory Material's Manager assignment had ended I returned to my corporate job. One day shortly after my return I was in the restroom standing at a urinal. I heard someone come up and take the urinal next to me. I turned my head to see who it was and found I was standing next to the VP of Purchasing, that is, the man who had initially hired the recently fired Materials Manager.

He turned his head to me and said something to the effect that "the recent situation could have been more easily handled if I had reported directly to him on what I had found." I doubted this since if I had done so, I didn't think it likely that if the issue would have been brought to light since it might have resulted in his initial hiring decision being questioned.

I replied, "When I took the interim Materials Manager job I was told that I would temporarily be reporting to the Division's Purchasing Director. Consequently, I had reported the issue not to my corporate chain of command but through the Divisional hierarchy."

He didn't reply and we both finished *our business*. But I could not keep from smiling as I left the restroom.

He and I never really got along after that. On the other hand, as people came to learn what had happened and understand the role I had played in getting the guy fired, I received congratulations from many of my colleagues.

## Summary

A person from outside the company was hired for a Materials Manager position. He took unethical actions to enhance his image within the purchasing community. I was able to document his indiscretions which formed the basis for him being fired from our company.

## Change Rating

*Evolutionary*. It resulted in getting rid of one rotten apple and set an example that this type of behavior would not be tolerated going forward.

## Lessons Learned

- The situation I had discovered could not be considered *nit-picking*. It was plainly wrong on a larger scale. Based on my personal and professional beliefs I knew the issue could not be allowed to stand and fester, so I acted, exposing myself to the risk of retribution. Such a blatant deception had, never to my knowledge, happened within the purchasing function of our corporation. In the end I found it was better to have done the right thing than to as the factory manager had suggested, dismiss the matter.

- If the suspicious issue you discover does not seem to be of great importance, the best thing is to probably let it slide. Yet it is important to be on the watch for bigger unethical behavior by the person in question.

On the other hand, if the issue could negatively affect the best interests of your company, you must act.

# As Chief Procurement
# Officer

# CHAPTER 36

# A Poor Alignment

Having *retired* from my first employer I consulted for 6 months at another corporate client. My task was to put together a business plan for the transformation of their purchasing strategy from a tactical to more strategic approach. Based on their acceptance of the plan I developed they offered the job as their Chief Purchasing Officer—a new position—which I accepted.

Since the hiring decision had been made with executive acceptance of the business plan I had developed, I expected that the transformation I had proposed would be supported.

Shortly after I started, I was invited to a meeting with the CFO. He asked me what I thought my main job was. I responded something to the effect of—*"Increasing purchasing's contribution of the competitiveness of the company outside of a sole focus on piece-price."*

The CFO replied that my primary responsibility should be to deliver purchased material cost reduction that he could feature at his quarterly meetings with stock analysts.

I replied that while we would continue to work on purchased material cost reductions, we would also be repurposing some department resources on the planned transformation.

He replied (and I'll always remember this moment).

*Your business plan was a nice academic study. Unfortunately, it wasn't based on current industrial realities.*

He ended up by saying that, in his opinion, all purchasing resources should be focused on reducing purchased material expenditures.

The above led to a very spirited verbal interchange.

This statement made it clear to me that the CFO was primarily focused on short-term results—hence the moniker *Short-Shrift*—which meant he wouldn't be supportive in the implementation of my business plan.

## Summary

There are always those who will resist change. One reason is that they don't feel comfortable operating outside of standard norms. In this case, the CFO refused to operate outside of his current perspective which, though it may have made his job easier, was not good for the longer-term competitiveness of the company.

## Change Rating

No change here, hence no Change Rating.

## Lessons Learned

- Managers don't always have the interests of their employer as their chief concern. Rather, they look to preserve processes they are comfortable with and/or focus their efforts on just the functional area they are responsible for. These managers should be resisted and their strategy exposed.

# CHAPTER 37

# Payment Terms from a Personal Perspective

At a CEO staff meeting it was *suggested* by Short-Shrift that I increase our supplier payment terms to 100 days from the current 30 day norm. It was clear I was being asked to play the role of the *bad guy* rather than that of a win-win collaborator. I asked what the basis for his suggestion was. He replied that he had industry intelligence that our primary competitor had just raised theirs to 100 days. Rather than agreeing or rejecting the idea in front of the CEO and his staff, I said I would investigate the matter and come back the following week with a recommendation.

## Gathering Intelligence

It turned out that there were many purchased part and/or assembly suppliers that were sourced from by both our competitors and us. I connected with a few of them and found out that the competitor had changed his payment terms to 60 days, not 100. I then asked them whether this change would affect the business relationship with that of other customers, explaining that I was being put under pressure to change our terms to match those of the competitors. Their common response was that going forward they would work with those firms on a commercial—not collaborative—basis. For instance, they would start charging for goods and services that they had previously provided at no *charge*—such as for prototype parts—and become more forceful in price negotiations.

At the next CEO staff meeting I reported that our competitor had extended payment term to 60, not 100 days. Instead of being embarrassed by this news, Short-Shrift immediately grabbed onto it and said that if we changed to 100 day payment terms it would give us a financial competitive advantage.

I replied that instead of that we should keep our terms at 30 days, telling the group that it would give us a more sustainable competitive advantage since we would be seen as a preferred customer based on the results of the survey I had done across a sample of common suppliers. Otherwise, I said, it would likely set-up an antagonistic relationship between us and our supply-base. Short-Shrift replied in a rather frosty tone that "it was my job to make sure that this didn't happen."

The CEO could see that our discussion was getting out of hand and tried to mediate the issue by saying we'd take the middle ground and just match the payment terms of our competitor.

I was in no position to challenge this and so sent out a communication to the supply-base announcing our changed payment terms.

## Summary

Many OEM executives don't understand the dynamics and benefits of managing suppliers in a win-win collaborative manner. Consequently, the CFO was more concerned in driving for quick-hit financial results that could be featured at his quarterly investor meetings benefits than putting strategies in place that could deliver higher, more sustainable benefits over time.

## Change Rating

*Tweaking*, since I was only partly successful in averting a portion of the negative impact extending supplier payment terms would have had on the corporation.

## Lessons Learned

- Extending supplier payment terms will likely cost an OEM customer more over the course of time than treating them as collaborating partners.
- Stand up for your suppliers internally when it makes business sense. If you are caught in a situation where you have little choice but to implement a program that will negatively affect your suppliers, attempt to mediate the negative impact on them.

# CHAPTER 38

# Extreme Frustration

I had become Chief Procurement Officer of a company comprised of four Divisions, two with multiple factories. They all used various highly engineered components and tended to purchase them from the same suppliers. Our Divisions individually bought their own components.

The result was that the company was not able to achieve the optimal pricing that was available by consolidating all company purchases.

## Case Study 1—Hydraulic Components

I had worked closely with my previous employer's primary hydraulic component supplier, which happened to be the same supplier sourced from by my new employer. Because of this past experience I had a strong understanding of how they conducted business. For instance, I knew they would be open to quoting on a consolidated corporate buy package *if there was some benefit in the deal for them.*

Our various Divisions did not typically have length-of-term contract commitments. I decided to offer the company's hydraulics supplier something all suppliers want, that is, a sole-source multiyear corporate contract. The hydraulic supplier agreed to this and proceeded to put together a consolidation package.

After a series of negotiating sessions we received a quote 8 percent lower than we were paying through the individual Division buy arrangement. What could be better than this? Unfortunately, I found there were internal problems that threw a wrench into the proposed agreement.

## The Pushback

Company Divisions were responsible for their own individual profitability. Although it was acknowledged that the negotiated agreement would result in an overall cost reduction for the corporation, it would not do so for all Divisions. Consequently, this change had the potential to look like those Divisions were lagging in cost-reduction performance, possibly making them look less effective compared with the ones who would get reduced pricing.

This should not have been a problem. Bonus parameters were set by the Short-Shrift and approved by a company's Board of Directors. In my experience up to that point I hadn't previously met a CFO—or Board— that would stand in the way of improving overall corporate financial results. In this instance, however, I found that Short-Shrift had no intention of *fiddling* (as he called it) with the current compensation packages.

The consolidation never went forward.

I wasn't speechless but probably should have been. This experience led to an ongoing rift between me and Short-Shrift. It also created silos between corporate purchasing and some Divisional Presidents such that future collaboration with them was limited during the remainder of my time with the corporation.

## Case Study 2

Another example like the one above also happened while I worked at this company. In this case, however, the resistance was due to a personal grudge one Divisional Manager had with a particular supplier.

Being a bit stubborn I made a proposal like what had been made with hydraulic components. Specifically, I suggested that all fastener purchases be made as a corporate buy. Again, up to this point, they had been purchased independently by each Division. The proposal made a lot of sense since not only would we likely get a cost reduction to the corporation but we would also likely receive additional *perks* such as supplier production line fastener stocking/management and not being invoiced for fasteners until they were assembled onto our products.

I was also able to make the argument that such arrangements were becoming an industry standard and that, in fact, one of our competitors had already implemented such a program.

The corporate purchasing function put a consolidated package out for bid, and we got a very favorable quote from a well-established hardware distributor, as well as their agreement to the two business perks mentioned above. I felt pretty good about the whole situation since I had worked with this supplier at my previous employer and there they provided ongoing high levels of tactical performance.

In return I had agreed that we commit to a multiyear, sole-source contract so that the supplier could feel they had also benefited from the business arrangement. The supplier agreed to the contract.

The result of the proposal was an overall 5 percent price reduction—a savings well into six figures—along with the other internal cost-reduction perks cited above. It had also resulted in a cost savings for all the corporation's Divisions. Because of this, I felt the main concern of the previously proposed hydraulic component consolidation proposal had been removed.

I was successful in getting three of our corporate Divisions to buy into the deal, but a fourth would not agree to participate.

## Pushback, Redux

I wondered why and discussed it with the dissenting Division's VP of Manufacturing, who also had responsibility for their purchasing function. He explained that his Division previously had a sole-source agreement with the supplier in question and that the supplier had, in fact, performed well.

He then informed me that a couple of years ago they had decided to put their fastener business out for *bid* in a real-time, online Dutch Auction. His hope was to be able to retain the incumbent supplier yet use the auction to leverage lower pricing from it.

The incumbent supplier refused to participate in the auction. This greatly *miffed* the Manufacturing Manager since it undercut his hoped-for result. He went ahead with the auction, but, for all intents and purchases, did not gain any cost advantage. And he did not get the perks that would have resulted in additional internal cost reductions. He also had to manage and expend resources in making the change from his incumbent supplier to the new one.

So, because of a personnel *tiff*, the Divisional VP vetoed the proposed contract. Because of this, the corporate deal fell through.

I was speechless and should have been quiet but couldn't help myself, increasing the environment of conflict between myself and the other corporate executives.

## Other Lost Opportunities

Similarly, corporate purchasing put together another money-saving deal for another commodity—steel—but for a variety of Divisional-related reasons we were not able to proceed with its implementation. I made a bit of a stink over this, too.

## Summary

I was hired by a large corporation as their Chief Procurement Officer and immediately saw the potential for some quick-hit cost reductions through consolidation of overall corporate requirements. In the first case it was blocked by an internal compensation structure and a reluctance to modify it. In the second case, the blockage was due to a petty grudge a Divisional Manager of manufacturing had against a particular supplier.

## Change Rating

None, hence no Change Rating.

## Lessons Learned

- CFOs tend to hold the most sway in Corporate America today. As a result, I came to understand that it is very difficult to challenge CFO stonewalling, even with a financially sound business case.

- When Divisions are set up to compete with each other their executives focus only on their own financial results. The only way this can be changed is by changing their performance metrics. In this case, the CFO, who had set up that competitive environment in the first place, had no interest in changing it.
- Vindictiveness—personnel pettiness—has no place in business. The best approach to addressing this is to give it visibility. In some cases, that approach will fail. Managers who make decisions based on it should be fired.
- I had gone to the CEO with my concerns. He deferred to the judgment of his CFO.

# As a Consultant

# CHAPTER 39

# An Unexpected Player

When I became a consultant I would often begin my engagement prior to finalizing a contract. Because of this I wasn't worried when I didn't finalize one with a new Fortune 100 client prior to starting my work with them. This seemed ok until I received a phone call from a *third party* that wanted to discuss payment terms. They told me that my client had outsourced its Accounts Payable function to his company and that they were contacting me to determine the length of time between the point when my services were rendered and the point when I wanted to receive payment. I replied that while I would like immediate payment I would accept 30-day terms.

His reply was that my client had standard 120-day payment terms with their suppliers but that his company was able to give payment options. For instance, if I wanted 30-day payment terms I would need to accept a 15 percent reduction in payment. He outlined a few other options, such as a 10 percent reduction for 60-day terms, but I wasn't really listening.

After he was done talking I told him that he should connect with my now *former* client and let them know I would reject any terms that would not pay me—in full—within 30 days and, without that, was withdrawing my services.

## Potential Client Follow-up

Wanting to make sure the now "potential" client got the straight truth about my decision, I telephoned my company contact and told her of my recent conversation with their outsourced third-party Accounts Payable vendor where they, in effect, intended to have me pay a fee to them without their adding value to the consulting services I was offering.

I also asked whether when larger consulting firms negotiated contracts with the third party. In other words, were they treated in the same way I had been? I was told "no."

## The Outcome

My contact called back the next day and said they would offer the payment terms I required. My experience led me to believe that whoever in my client's company that had come up with the idea, thinking it to *entice* suppliers to reduce their margins, really didn't understand the ins and outs of effective supplier management.

## Summary

A new client had outsourced their Accounts Payable function to an outside third party. This company had been given license to discount payments—where they would get a percentage of the discount—in return for shorter payment terms.

I threatened to withdraw my consulting services unless they honored my 30-day payment terms and, as a result, got to deal directly with my client who opted to meet them.

## Change Rating

*Incremental*, since my client still retained the third-party Accounts Payable service for other suppliers. On the other hand, there must have been significant pushback by the client's supply-base since I heard the arrangement was discontinued after a couple of years.

## Lessons Learned

- Despite abandoning their thirty-party extending payment terms strategy I had no doubt that it had damaged the relationship it had with its supply-base. There is a basic supply management–related maxim that many OEMs forget. That is "If you treat your suppliers in a win-lose manner, sooner or later they will be in position to be able put you on the losing side."

- My experience with my client's extending payment terms foray should have been a red flag. In my entire career—both in corporate America and consulting—I have not seen a more fearful supply-base. Supply-base problems—mainly quality and delivery—became so endemic that they received extensive media coverage.

- After a 3-year engagement, consulting impact was minimal. Change proposals—backed up by Proof-of-Concept pilot results—were not adopted by the client. This, in spite of the U.S. Department of Commerce learning of them and inviting my client to report on them as a keynote speaker at a White House Supply Management Conference.

# CHAPTER 40

# Effective Consulting

When I began to think about starting up a consultancy there were two primary questions I wanted to explore. First, standard consulting practice. Second, the effectiveness—cost versus positive, quantifiable financial impact—of current consulting services. I knew I would be competing against existing consultancies and needed to understand how I could differentiate my services from those of competitors.

I decided the primary clientele to target would be OEMs. After all, I had spent the better part of my professional career working as an OEM purchasing executive and had a good *change agent* track record in the purchasing arena.

My prior experiences with consultancies were with those hired by my employer and those hired by suppliers I had worked with. I expected to be competing with larger consultancies and, based on this, made the following observations.

1. They tend to assign several employees to a customer engagement, many of which are marginally necessary.
2. They typically room-and-board at top-of-the-line hotels and restaurants—non–value-added costs—which their clients are expected to pay for.
3. The onsite consultants, themselves, have little or no actual purchasing experience. This is especially true relative to a manager or executive with a background in purchasing. Advanced degrees in business and so on aren't an effective replacement for experience.
4. To address this deficiency they train their employers to implement a single cookie-cutter engagement process. This means that the same steps are followed client after client, regardless of individual customer circumstances.

5. Cookie-cutter implementations tend to focus on revision of organizational job descriptions and headcount. While such areas may (or may not) need attention down the road, they do not typically meet the expectations of a client, who wants shorter-term, quantifiable positive financial impacts.

Based on these observations, I decided to structure my consulting services as follows.

- Minimize out-of-pocket expenses. For instance, I would stay at mid-priced motels or, if the engagement looked to be over a longer term, rent an apartment, whose monthly rent would be significantly lower than 30 days at a mid-priced motel.
- Operate as a company of *one*, relying on my experience in development of a World-Class Supply-Base, which should be the goal of all purchasing functions.
- Set my daily fee below that of the larger consultancies. This would be possible since I would not have employees to pay, overheads to offset, or the need to achieve organizational profitability goals.
- Tailor client-specific strategies and practices that would lead to quick-hit high-impact improvements.

I had personal experience to back up the points in the above two lists. One of my clients had engaged a midsized consultancy for 7 months with very little to show for it. Based on a recommendation from a former client I was brought in to operate side by side—but independently—during my engagement. The existing consultancy operated exactly as described above.

## Summary

I was hired to consult with a client that had had been working with a midsized consultancy, who had four full-time employees onsite working on their project. Three of four had no purchasing experience, while the fourth had never been a purchasing manager or executive.

The midsized consultant operated with a cookie-cutter approach. My approach was to tailor my recommendations to client. I was much more effective, and the other consultancy lost their contract after a few months.

## Change Rating

*Revolutionary.* First, it is rare for a single person consultancy to displace a larger, more established consultant. I was simply more effective. Second, I have never seen or even heard of my consulting process—which ties recommendation to both personal performance metrics and those of other functional areas (see next chapter)—employed in obtaining a client or implemented in the engagement.

## Lessons Learned

- Potential clients usually need to be taught how the purchasing function can positively impact their company financials above and beyond material cost reduction.
- It is an effective strategy to tie personal performance metrics to those impacts.
- Red flags should go up when consultants advocate cookie-cutter approaches as their primary improvement strategy.

# CHAPTER 41

# Assessment of Client Needs

I've found that most managers and executives are more likely to support consultancy engagements if they see them as leading to improvements to their own personal performance metrics. However, what is often not understood within an organization, is how purchasing can positively impact an organization's other functional departments and in doing so, improve individual performance metrics outside of purchasing.

Consequently, my first goal was to educate a potential client on how changes in purchasing strategies and practices can improve Exhibit-level Operational Metrics and, as well, tie them to personnel and departmental performance metrics.

In approaching a potential client—after performing due diligence through publicly available documents, such as annual reports—I would ask that they commit to a 2-day proposal engagement. On the first day I would tour their factory, meet with organizational principals, and generically review with them the types of positive impacts from my past consulting engagements. Then I would meet with my main supplier contact—usually a Materials Manager—for a discussion of the cost of engagement versus the potential cost-reduction benefit.

I would ask this individual what their personnel and departmental performance goals were. The typical answer was purchased material cost reduction, On-time Delivery, and Quality.

My next question would be to ask for a copy of what their organizational Exhibit metrics, that is, those that are used by corporate to track and measure unit efficiency and effectiveness. I would then take them back to my hotel for study and based on them, create a proposal.

## A Tailor-made Engagement

The following day I would outline to my contact how a change in purchasing strategies and practice could positively impact personal and departmental performance metrics, as well as those of other factory functional areas.

This meant that, for instance, having a more agile and reliable supply-base could both lower the need for stocks of raw material and have the potential to increase Customer Fill Rates, reducing the need for prebuilt, prepositioned finished goods inventory.

Raw material stocks are typically part of a Manufacturing Department's performance metrics, while Customer Fill Rates and the amount of prebuilt, prepositioned finished goods inventory are typically included in a Marketing Department's performance metrics. Because of this, a supplier agility initiative would likely gain support from other functional departments.

There are many other examples of how changes in purchasing strategies and practice can positively impact a company's financials above and beyond material cost reduction. To deliver them requires a World-Class Supply-Base able to cost-effectively react to *short-fuse* schedule changes.

This will require adding a supplier performance metric of *true* lead-time and using it as a factor at the same level of importance as material cost reduction in making sourcing decisions. Supplier development resources would also be needed to support a phased-in supplier *true* lead-time reduction initiative.

The above types of impacts will likely require changes to executive-level perceptions of purchasing's strategic potential. Part of my role—and that of my primary client contact—is to educate them on this.

## Summary

Large consultancies often focus as much—or more—on improving their own bottom lines than on client cost reduction and operational improvement. It takes experienced purchasing personnel—at the managerial or executive level—to tailor client-specific strategies and practices focused on both short-term and ongoing positive and quantifiable financial impact. To do this, a consultant must educate potential clients on the impacts that purchasing can have on Exhibit-Level and Managerial/Executive level performance metrics.

Relative to the engagement cited above where I was essentially competing with another consultancy, I outperformed them in every possible way—to the point, in fact, that their corporate head of operations wanted me to join their firm and co-manage the ongoing engagement. I declined. They were soon dismissed from their engagement.

## Change Rating

*Evolutionary.* I have never seen my approach used by any other consultancy that has proved itself so effective in promoting the strategic value of purchasing above and beyond material cost reduction.

## Lessons Learned

- Educating executive- and managerial-level employees on how purchasing can positively contribute to that bottom line—above and beyond material cost reduction—is critical in convincing a potential client that engaging you as a consultant will increase company competitiveness. Tying this knowledge to improvement of their own personal performance metrics can be a successful strategy for achieving this.
- Effective managerial and/or executive experience in purchasing—as well as an education at the *school of hard knocks*—is needed for a consultant to tailor a consulting engagement that will optimize purchasing's contributions to an organization's bottom line.
- Producing improvement in performance metrics in other functional areas—for instance, as described in the manufacturing and marketing examples above—can further convince a client that purchasing should be regarded as a strategic and not a tactical function.

- The addition of nontraditional purchasing source selection and performance metrics will be required to deliver these results. They include *true* lead-time reduction.
- The above changes will position purchasing to have a *seat at the table* when decisions on strategy and metrics are being made.

# PART 3

# Afterward

# CHAPTER 42

# Endgame

It is not often that an employee has the opportunity to be involved in delivering a fundamental change to corporate strategy. I was fortunate enough to be able to live that experience. It was gratifying, both professionally and personally. Making the necessary changes to strategy and practice necessitated years of heavy lifting to make the purchasing changes required to achieve this. Many of these changes are detailed in previous chapters of this book. In this chapter, I will outline how they were put together to deliver an epic positive financial impact.

## The Financial Homerun

The reduction of supplier *true* lead-times as the basis for our supplier development strategy was explained and outlined earlier in this book. As were the positive impact(s) that supplier development engagements can have on individual supplier competitiveness. As previously mentioned, prior to our decision to market our products through the Big Box marketing channel our supplier development function had engaged all 80 of our strategic—noncommodity—suppliers and facilitated reducing their *true* lead-times by an average of 80 percent!

## The Challenge

Big Box Stores provide their suppliers with forecast *guidance* but do not commit to buying unsold inventory due to variations in market demand. In fact, they expect suppliers to react to short-fuse schedule changes by delivering the needed product to their stores within seven days; that is, their target is to hold only a weeks' worth of inventory so as to not lose sales by not having *on hand* what is currently selling.

# The Solution

As it turns out our *true*-lead-time reduction initiative was exactly what was needed to facilitate our Division's move into the Big Box marketing channel. You may wonder why the 80 percent reduction in *true* lead-times was so important to this initiative. There are two approaches for manufacturers in supporting sales when demand varies from what was forecast.

The one most frequently used by our competition was to rely on large stocks of prebuilt, prepositioned finished goods inventory of every SKU such that it would be on hand and available to satisfy Big Box Store order fulfillment expectations.

Prebuilt finished product inventory were especially needed in our industry since its products had a highly cyclical sales season. Consequently, sourcing with suppliers unable to support short-fuse schedule changes and deliver parts within the timeframe a customer was willing to wait for a product can significantly reduce customer fill rates, i.e. sales.

Building inventory ahead of demand is a risky strategy since it may not include the needed volume for individual SKUs or result in leftover product, leaving the OEM in the lurch for unneeded inventory.

The prebuilt finished product inventory approach was, in fact, used by all of our competition. This was necessary because most of their purchased parts were sourced with foreign suppliers, that is, those with inherently long *true* lead-times.

The second approach is through development of a World-Class Supply-Base that had the production agility to cost-effectively react to short-fuse changes in production schedule. In our supplier development world we had created one!

Our need for order fulfillment flexibility required all suppliers be located domestically. Needless to say, this was a major change to the typical sourcing strategy since most OEMs—including our competition—preferred to chase lower piece-prices by sourcing with overseas suppliers.

The implication was that if our suppliers had the capability—capacity and order fulfillment agility—to support our Big Box customer's order fulfillment needs—it would tremendously reduce our dependence on prebuilt finished product inventory, leading to a significant cost-related competitive advantage.

## A Plan Coming to Fruition

The initial Big Box customer forecasts came in at 175,000 units, which was double the number of what one of our similar products had sold through our dealerships just the year before. So, we were very happy. It seemed that our new marketing strategy would pay off handsomely.

Customer-demand forecasts went up weekly in the 6-month run-up to our cyclical sales season, eventually ending up at double that forecast.

We were able react to the changes in customer product preferences well within our 3-month sales season, while still maintaining high Customer Fill Rates.

## The Impact

As stated above, the initial forecast came in at 175,000 units. Customer demand eventually was double that, that is, 350,000. We were able to satisfy 343,000 of those orders—in other words, 91 percent of the un-forcasted demand which translated to a customer fill rate of 98%, an unheard-of feat both within our company and across our industry in general.

Our Big Box Store customer benefited by being able to satisfy almost all of the demand for our products. In addition to this benefit, our Division benefited significantly based on the higher profitability of Incremental sale of product units by 173,000 beyond the projected numbers. For instance, overheads are assigned in setting product pricing. Sales above forecast result in *windfall* profitability. Why? Because sales above the initial forecast have no overhead costs assigned with them, increasing profit margin along the lines of 30 percent. Selling those 173,000 extra units delivered tens of millions of dollars in profits above what had been forecast to our Division's bottom line.

By the way, suppliers of parts for these products also experienced similar windfall profits. In addition, we were able to avoid having to prebuild $890,000 in finished goods inventory, another source of tremendous savings.

## An Epic Change in Corporate Purchasing Strategy and Practice

Financial results like this could not be ignored. It took two additional years, but in the end, *true* lead-time became a supplier sourcing and performance criteria within our company. In a pragmatic move, this led to an increasing pricing penalty correlated to higher supplier *true* lead-times in the company's Total Cost of Ownership formula. I have never heard of this taking place outside of our company.

## Summary

Our Division had decided to change our marketing strategy by selling product through Big Box merchandisers. Our competition supported unanticipated market demand by prebuilding and positioning finished product such that they had ability to ship to their Big Box customers from on-hand inventory.

We understood that we could only obtain a competitive advantage by significantly reducing the need for prebuilt, prepositioned finished product inventory through in-house and supply chain manufacturing agility. It was recognized that we had this capability because the supplier development assistance we had provided reduced their *true* lead-times.

When demand came in double of what had been initial forecast, 98 percent of it was met due to having supplier-based order fulfillment capability. This not only resulted in significant windfall profits. It also justified adding supplier development resources and raised the visibility of the importance of supplier *true* lead-time in the assessment of supplier capability and supplier performance evaluation!

Consequently, *true* lead-time was given the same level of consideration in source selection as piece-price, added to a supplier's quoted price in my company's Total Cost of Ownership formula. That is, the longer a supplier's *true* lead-time, the higher the price penalty.

## Change Rating

*Revolutionary.* No explanation needed!

## Lessons Learned

- Fundamental change in business strategies and processes requires a lot of perseverance, heavy lifting, and a longer-term commitment. But it can be highly rewarding.
- The necessary heavy lifting cannot be accomplished by typical purchasing strategies and staff. It requires adding manufacturing-savvy supplier development resources to the purchasing function in support of the new strategies.
- Populating supplier development with individuals having educational backgrounds that align with strategic goals is important. In this case, it was advanced Master's-prepared Industrial Engineers whose curriculum was based on the axiom *time is money.*

# CHAPTER 43

# World-Class Suppliers

## What It Means to Have a World-Class Supply-Base

What does the term World-Class Supply-Base imply? This question cannot be answered without first understanding what being a World-Class Supplier means. The answer to this isn't as simple as it might seem.

The short answer to this might be that a World-Class Supplier is one that operates *without waste*. I have yet to see a supplier—or OEM for that matter—that can say they have no waste. Yet there are companies that classify themselves as World-Class.

No matter how Lean a supplier is operationally, delivery time should be considered waste and included when assessing a supplier's *Leanness*. So, unless an OEM can *snap its fingers* and purchased parts magically appear, all suppliers have some level of waste. And as previously pointed out in this book, suppliers with longer *true* lead-times should be considered less Lean, regardless of the *Leanness* of their internal operations.

Another possible definition of a World-Class Supplier is one whose parts have *Six Sigma quality*, are *delivered on time*, and are *competitive pricewise*. Of course, quality and competitive pricing matter, but what does *deliver on time* mean? Is it delivering parts in time to support an OEM's production schedule? No. But if not, what does it mean?

## Market Dynamics and Customer Demand

In my experience, OEM's production schedules rarely align with customer demand. Why? Because schedules are based on forecasts, and there is always error in a forecast, sometimes a lot. So even if a supplier appears to be able to support an OEM customer's production schedule, that schedule may not align with market demand and need to be revised.

So, what is required to mediate forecast error while relying on minimum waste? Short *true* lead-times. This is particularly important in consumer markets where varying customer demand is difficult to forecast, which means that a supplier with longer *true* lead-times may not be able react to their OEM customer's short-fuse schedule changes.

A good example of this is when forecasts dramatically underestimate demand for certain Christmas products and, as a result, potential sales are lost and the hopes of children for popular presents aren't realized.

Bottom line, neither an OEM or supplier can be considered World-Class if their forecasts have error and a product's overall *true* lead-time doesn't align with varying customer demand.

A World-Class Supply-Base, then, might be one where all suppliers that comprise it have Six Sigma quality, competitive pricing, and the manufacturing agility needed to support variations in market demand that is different than what was forecast.

So, what should be the definition of a World-Class Supply-Base?

A World-Class Supply-Base *is one that can not only deliver Six Sigma quality and competitive pricing but also has short enough true lead-times such that they can align their production with the dynamics of the market their OEM's customer participates in without relying on excessive waste.*

# CHAPTER 44

# The North Star

As you've read through the book you've undoubtedly come to under-stand that I believe the goal of all purchasing functions should be the development of a World-Class Supply-Base. When I first started on my purchasing journey I didn't recognize all of the changes that would be needed to develop one.

Through my *change agent* activity, though, I came to understand that many changes in purchasing perspective, strategy and process are needed to deliver one. I'll outline some of these in the following table, comparing **Traditional** practices to the **New Paradigm** ones.

| Traditional | New Paradigm |
|---|---|
| 1. Setting supplier performance standards and giving feedback on performance are sufficient for OEM supplier development involvement | An OEM's willingness to provide suppliers the same level of technical and resource support they would receive if they were departments in the OEM's own factory |
| 2. Changing suppliers to chase lower pricing is an efficient long-term supply management strategy | Only source with suppliers who have the *true* lead-times necessary to support the demand dynamics of the market a customer's product is to be marketed in |
| 3. Suppliers bidding in real-time online auctions to retain current business | OEMs assisting suppliers to lower costs through print reviews and supplier development support |
| 4. OEMs' broad-brush annual supply-base price-reduction goals | Individually tailored price-reduction goals based on supplier specifics, such as product type, that is, wireform vs. stamping, and their current state of *Lean-ness*; that is, the Leaner a supplier is, the lower the cost-reduction potential |
| 5. Suppliers are experts in the manufacture of their products. OEM customers can contribute little toward improving their operations | OEM customers help suppliers reduce cost by introducing them to, and assisting them in implementing, modern manufacturing practices |

| Traditional | New Paradigm |
|---|---|
| 6. Challenging suppliers with mandated price reductions helps them by pushing them to become Leaner | Prices go down when costs go down. Imposing price reduction mandates tends to make suppliers more anorexic than anything else |
| 7. Supplier performance metrics measuring their impact on an OEM's operation are best for assessing supplier capability | Supplier performance metrics that more closely align with their customer's ability to support market demand are best for assessing supplier performance |
| 8. Applying leverage in win-lose negations is the most effective strategy for getting ongoing price reductions | Collaboration with suppliers in win-win negotiations is effective in both delivering short-term price reductions and creating the potential to reduce internal waste at the OEM customer's operation |
| 9. Suppliers should be judged by their Quality, Delivery, and Price Reduction performance results | It is important to understand how a supplier produces their performance results, that is, through Lean manufacturing or not, especially in understanding their potential for future price reductions |
| 10. Managing suppliers from a desk is an efficient way to deal with them | Onsite supplier visits are necessary to gain an understanding of how to tailor supplier-specific management plans |
| 11. Considering purchasing as strictly a cost center | Considering purchasing both as a cost center and a revenue center. |

It is unlikely that all changes from **Traditional** to **New Paradigm** practices can occur simultaneously. Successfully tackling them one or two at a time can set the stage for further change within your organization.

Developing a World-Class Supply-Base will take many years. It is not a *quick-hit* initiative.

But as Henry Ford once said:

*Changes that require little effort are usually not worth the effort.*

# Glossary

**Agility:** See *True* Lead-time (below).

**Big Box Merchandiser:** A retail store that occupies an enormous amount of physical space and offers a variety of products to its customers. These stores achieve economies of scale by focusing on products that have the potential for large sales volumes. Because of this, the profit margin for each product can be lowered, which results in very competitively priced goods. The term "Big Box" is derived from the store's physical appearance.

**Business Consulting:** A business consultant is an individual who is a catalyst for change toward improving a client's competitive market position.

**Chief Procurement Officer:** Is responsible for the management, administration, and supervision of the company's acquisition of materials and IM&S. They also may be in charge of buying capital equipment. It is a Chief Procurement Officer's responsibility to oversee negotiation of prices and contracts. In more progressive corporations, CPOs report directly to the CEO.

**Collaboration:** The process of two or more people, entities, or organizations working together to complete a task or achieve a goal. Collaboration is similar to cooperation. Teams that work collaboratively look for win-win results.

**Commercial:** The practice of making one's living by engaging in buying or selling for profit, without concern about the profitability of any other party involved in the transaction.

**Cookie-Cutter:** Is when the same strategy and/or process is always used in approaching a particular task, not paying enough attention to individual differences or needs.

**Con Artist:** A person who cheats or tricks others by persuading them to believe something that is not true.

**Customer Fill Rate:** The percentage of time an OEM has product in stock to sell when a customer wants to buy it. This is a metric that ties directly to lost sales.

**Division:** A system in which a company segments and operates its businesses through individual organizations called Divisions, each of which is focused on managing specific products in specific markets.

**Ethics:** Principles that govern a person's behavior relative to moral right and wrong, or moral good and bad. Personal ethics govern an individual's behavior in the conduct of an activity.

**Extended Enterprise:** A business perspective in which an OEM regards its supply chain as part of its overall operation akin to their own internal departments. This perspective implies a different strategy for management of noncommodity (engineered part and component) suppliers.

**Firefighter:** In business parlance it is a term often used to describe a person who rushes to mediate a problem but, in doing so, does not discover or address its root cause. This implies that even if a problem has been "fixed" in the present, it has as much risk of occurring in the future as it had before the firefighting took place.

**Flexibility:** See *True* Lead-time (below).

**Forecast:** A statement of what is expected to happen in the future, especially related to a specific point in time or period of time. In business, this term is often related to market demand for specific products.

**Function:** An activity or purpose natural—or intended—for a specific thing. In business, this term often relates to office and operational activities.

**Greenfield Site:** In business, this term describes an area or structure that is being completely repurposed or has never been previously used. Greenfield sites allow for the implementation of manufacturing models designed for specific purposes with an intent to install Best-in-Class operations.

**Holding Companies:** Have as a specific purpose to buy, control, and manage subsidiary companies in which it holds majority ownership. They work to improve each of their captured companies' financial spreadsheets—at least superficially—and then to sell them for more than they paid for them, that is, flip them, within the shortest turnaround time possible.

**Inspection Approvals:** Inspection in manufacturing is the process of examining and/or evaluating parts and components. For suppliers, a satisfactory final inspection is required to receive their OEM customer's approval for shipment of their product to them. For OEM customers, their own internal Receiving Inspection department may have to approve incoming shipments prior to delivery to their point of use.

**Incremental Sales:** Related to windfall profits. Product cost is based on material cost, labor cost, and overheads. The first two costs are variable and directly related to the number of products produced. Overhead is a fixed cost based on a yearly forecast. Sales of product above the forecast, then, means products having sold without overhead costs assigned to them. This can result in a doubling or tripling of profit per machine.

**Indirect Materials and Services (IM&S):** Materials and supplies that are considered commodities. They also include services rendered by outside suppliers onsite at a customer's facility.

**Market Demand:** Market demand is the total quantity of goods or services that, at any one time, consumers want to buy. Forecasts are tied to market demand since they are meant to predict specific periods of customer demand.

**Nemeses:** An agent of someone's or something's downfall, based on a long-standing rivalry. For instance, in the Star Wars movies, Darth Vader was a nemesis of Luke Skywalker.

**Order Fulfillment:** Refers to a process by which a product that has been manufactured and delivered to a customer.

**Original Equipment Manufacturer:** A company that manufactures a product that, upon completion, is ready for sale to a customer.

**Outlier:** A person, thing, or fact that is extremely different from others in their category, such that they should not be used in drawing general conclusions.

**Outside Purchased Product:** A product manufactured by one OEM for sale to another OEM, ready for sale to an end-use customer. The product in question is branded and otherwise tailored to fill a gap in the second OEM's product line.

**Pilot Project:** Is an initial small-scale implementation that is used to prove to an organization the viability of a new idea or process, identifying risks and deficiencies.

**Positional Negotiations:** See Win-Lose negotiations.

**Prebuilt Finished Product:** Inventory that is used to fulfill Customer Fill Rates when an OEM's customer product is either out of stock and they do not have the inherent capability and/or flexibility within their *extended enterprise* (see above)— not just within their own factories—to do so. Finished goods inventory is costly to build and maintain and can negatively affect company's financials, especially when demand doesn't materialize as forecast.

**Production Schedule:** A clearly defined timeframe for carrying out a series of processes or procedures. In business the term is typically linked to production of a finished product. When a schedule is based on an errant forecast, a schedule is often changed in an attempt to mediate that error for better market support.

**Proof-of-Concept Pilot Project:** Pilot project risks and deficiencies are addressed in a final concept trial, the success or failure of which typically leads either to full implementation or the discarding of the idea or process in question.

**Raw Material Safety Stock:** *Raw* refers to the materials that are used in the manufacture of finished products. *Safety Stocks* are used by an OEM customer to mediate the risk of a supplier not being able to deliver parts on time in order to support a production schedule.

**Response Time:** See *True* Lead-time (below).

**Strategic Sourcing:** An OEM purchasing department group that is responsible for the selection of strategic suppliers (see below). In many cases, once selected, a tactical purchasing group with responsibility for daily factory operations takes over the management of these suppliers.

**Strategic Supplier:** A supplier that would either be difficult or impossible to replace due to their intellectual property, patents, or manufacturing capabilities.

**Supplier Audits:** Are performed by customers to assess supplier operations to ensure that they meet certain manufacturing capability standards.

**True lead-time:** The typical amount of calendar time from when a manufacturing order is created through the critical-path until the first, single end-item of that order is delivered to the customer.

**Win-Lose Negotiations:** Negotiations where one—or all—parties have a goal of significantly increasing their own financial benefit at the expense of the other. In this case, they have little or no concern about the negative impact the results of the negotiations might have on any of the other parties.

**Win-Win Negotiations:** Negotiations that are conducted in a collaborate manner. A goal of win-win negotiations is to increase the "size of the pie" such that all negotiating parties benefit from the end-result.

**Zero-sum Game:** See "win-lose" negotiations.

# Index

www.ingramcontent.com/pod-product-compliance
Lightning Source LLC
Chambersburg PA
CBHW061151220326
41599CB00025B/4444